Utopian Bodies and the Politics of Transgression

The Library

Green

meet ir

form a

than b

explora

Here

intentic

the put

Lucy S

dilemm

Utopi

work. I

feminis

People

introdu

Lucy S

Notting

1996).

Utopian Bodies and
the Politics of Transgression

Lucy Sargisson

London and New York

First published 2000 by Routledge
2 Park Square, Milton Park, Abingdon, Oxon, OX14 4RN

Simultaneously published in the USA and Canada
by Routledge
29 West 35th Street, New York, NY 10001

Routledge is an imprint of the Taylor & Francis Group

Transferred to Digital Printing 2004

Typeset in Baskerville by Steven Gardiner Ltd

British Library Cataloguing in Publication Data
A catalogue record for this book is available
from the British Library

Library of Congress Cataloging in Publication Data
A catalog record for this book has been requested

ISBNs 0-415-21462-9 (hb)
      0-415-21463-7 (pb)

For Hilary Sargisson

Contents

Acknowledgements

This book is the product of research funded by the following grant-awarding bodies:

- The British Academy, whose overseas travel grant permitted me to attend a meeting of the Utopian Studies Society in Toronto. This was inspirational.
- The Economic and Social Research Council, to whom I am indebted for a year's study leave. This enabled me to visit the communities in question and to think and read.
- The University of Nottingham's Quick Response Fund financed a pilot project, from which came much useful material.

I owe debts of gratitude to all those who have read drafts of the following chapters. These include my friends and colleagues Chris Pierson, Andy Dobson, David Stevens, Lyman Sargent, Simon Tormey, Tom Moylan and the anonymous reviewer for Routledge as well as Clare Cummings and Simon Brown at the Findhorn Foundation. Thanks also go to Conrad Sargisson for his contributions on ecclesiastical property. The book would never have existed but for Caroline Wintersgill's faith in commissioning it and thanks are due also to Vicky Smith at Routledge. Friends have been important. These include the Keele girls: Pauline Weston, Teresa Steele and Kath McKeown; and Heather Orme, April Pidgeon, from Nottingham, as well as Ben Seel, Paul Tulley and Colin Rowan. Thanks to Laura Briggs and April Pidgeon for transcribing the interviews. Students of Nottingham University have been consistent in their enthusiasm for this project and colleagues in the School of Politics' Reading Group have challenged and maintained mental alertness. Thanks, too, to Paul Heywood.

Mostly though my thanks are due to those in the intentional communities for permitting me to visit, for talking to me and trusting me and for letting me into their homes and lives.

Introduction to utopian bodies

This book is about bodies of thought and bodies of people. It explores an approach to the world that is at once utopian and pragmatic. I call it transgressive utopianism. Transgressive utopianism is open-ended, slippery and glorious. Its aim is to enable the creative thought that I suggest is necessary to appropriately address some of the difficult questions and issues thrown up by contemporary political life. These questions include the attention to philosophical debates, fictions and high theory; personal decisions, choices, dreams, longings and desires; and the practical politics of action.

- What do we want?
- What do we believe to be wrong with the world?
- How can we best change it?
- How should we live?
- Given the world as it is, how can we best achieve our dreams and desires?

These questions are impossibly large and I make no claims to solve the problems that they raise. I am, however, concerned to attempt to address them. It seems to me that a plurality of voices is the best approach to take and this book is an attempt to begin a process in which this can occur. I therefore gather together a number of bodies that have concern with these questions. These are bodies of thought and bodies of people. My interpretation of the word 'body' is flexible. When considering bodies of thought a 'body' is read as a distinct mass. Elsewhere, the body is taken to be a group of individuals, organised for some purpose. Here, the focus is on what might be expected in a book on utopias: intentional communities. These are frequently taken to be attempts to create the concrete utopia: Heaven on Earth: the ideal society. I shall be suggesting that this is not actually a function of these communities.

The bodies, then, are green political thought, and deep ecology in particular; feminist theory; historical utopias; deconstructive theory; and ecological intentional communities. Attempts have been made also to make space for the fact that within these so-called bodies are tensions and conflicts and the voices evoked in this book are not simply taken to be representatives of 'a position'. There is a considerable porosity in the boundaries that separate these bodies, and exchange is encouraged throughout.

Transgressive utopianism can be frustrating and indeed will always frustrate desires for single answers and easy programs of action. It is an approach to the process and practice of theorising. Theory aims to explain and predict. As a theorist it is my business to make the complex comprehensible and therein lies a paradox because the kind of theory that this book advocates and practices makes this impossible. And, I suggest, it glories in this paradox. The resistance that this represents is not, however, wilful or obstinate. It is principled and aims at an account – or series of accounts – appropriate to the complexities of the world. This approach is not postmodern for the sake of being so; nor feminist; nor ecologist; nor utopian. Rather it is profoundly pragmatic. It is responsive to the 'real' world. By this I mean that it resists dogma. This is not to say that the approach taken here is value-free or objective. My own bias is apparent and owned. My influences come from all of the bodies referred to and also from the wider intellectual, cultural and social contexts of ideology, religion, gender, race and class.

The thinking offered here is transgressive in a particular way.

- It is internally subversive, which is to say that it challenges from within the aims and assumptions of the ground whence it comes (political theory, utopian philosophy, academic study, etc.).
- It is flexible and resistant to permanence and order and even while it constructs an account (of, e.g., 'politics') it accepts its own imminent dissolution. Nothing lasts forever in a changing environment.
- It is intentionally and deliberately utopian. The book asserts, contra popular assumptions, that a certain utopianism is essential to process and dynamism.

This is transgressive utopianism.

Transgressive utopianism is the product of an approach to utopian thinking that does not insist upon utopia as blueprint: utopia as the inscription of perfection. I first conceived of this phenomenon when writing *Contemporary Feminist Utopianism* (1996). I had noticed that feminist theory was marked by a certain utopianism, but also that this utopianism did not 'fit' into the prevailing definition of utopia as the blueprint of an ideal polity. Convinced that this was nonetheless utopianism that I perceived, I set about to review the utopian canon to see what I could find. I found that the blueprint model of utopia was wrong not only of contemporary feminisms, but also that it was inappropriate to many historical utopias. I set about reconceptualising utopia and formulated the idea of a utopianism that was transgressive in some way of the way in which our world is currently ordered. I found language to be one primary ordering factor and, in particular, the tradition

[margin handwritten note: How does it differ from a critical utopia]

of binary oppositional thought that erects hierarchies and associations of hierarchies that mediate our relation to the world. These things affect the way that we think about and relate to the world, and sustainable political change requires that we first enable ourselves to break free of mental constraints and think differently. Thinking genuinely differently is a process that cannot occur within existing constraints and so I suggest that we seek tools that enable a paradigm shift in consciousness.

Utopias – good places that are no place – are good places from whence to attempt this kind of thinking. They are outside the real world, but engage critically with it. They arise from discontent and attempt creative imaginings of how things might be better. They provide for bodies-of-thought spaces in which creativity is possible, they add momentum and resist the petrifaction to which academic minds are vulnerable. They give to social and political movements a sense of direction or vision. Utopias are ideal places in which to engage in the kind of thinking that I suggest is appropriate to the contemporary political environment.

Utopian thought works thus:

- It issues from political dissatisfaction and offers political critique.
- It articulates estrangement and offers an alternative perspective, from an alien (or new) space.
- It is creative and imaginative and often fictional.
- It has subversive and transformative potential.

Some utopian thought is significantly transgressive.

Again, whilst working on *Contemporary Feminist Utopianism* (and from the premise that our approach to the world affects that world and our conceptions of it) I found much of the utopianism of contemporary feminisms to operate in a specific manner. It transgresses, negates and destroys things that confine it. And, in so doing, it generates – issues – a space in which something different can occur: a utopian space. This I call new conceptual space. Multiplicity and a profound resistance to closure mark these spaces in feminist thought and fiction. There is no fullstop to the process of politics in this utopianism.

This then, briefly, is transgressive utopianism. Taking Thomas More's etymological pun as a base line, utopia is the good place (*eutopos*) that is no place (*outopos*). It is wild, unruly, rule-breaking thought that is politically driven and that expresses a profound discontent with the political present. It cannot be confined to one discipline as generic expectations are but another set of ordering structures that it rejects as invalid to its reality. It is, above all, resistant to closure and it celebrates process over product. Rather than construct a blueprint for the ideal polity, transgressive utopian thought engages with contemporaneous debate. This might be the equality/difference/diversity polemic of contemporary feminism, or the Church and State debate of 16th Century England, or the problems of constructing a politics appropriate to providing sustainable response to environmental degradation.

Transgressive utopian thought works thus:

- It breaks rules and confronts boundaries.
- It challenges paradigms.
- It creates new conceptual and political space.

In this space, creative thinking and activity is possible. Transgressive utopianism is critical utopianism in the sense developed by Tom Moylan (Moylan 1986). The critical utopia, says Moylan, is critical in two senses: first in the Enlightenment sense of critique, and second in the nuclear sense of critical mass. This mass he connects to what he calls a new historic bloc of opposition. *Contemporary Feminist Utopianism* looked at how transgressive utopianism can change the ways that we think. *Utopian Bodies* is concerned to address also questions of agency. Is it possible to change the ways that we think and act as political agents?

Utopian Bodies articulates a belief that different intellectual traditions should and can speak and listen to one another. This statement of interdisciplinarity steps also into an anti-disciplinary posture from which a new way of studying is emergent. In Chapter 1, the utopian canon, green political thought, feminist thought and deconstructive theory are introduced and established as bodies of thought for the purposes of this current study. Chapter 2 introduces the bodies of people. These come from Britain's ecology movement and comprise intentional communities, in which people have chosen to live together for some purpose beyond convenience or affection. Ground is sought on which these bodies might usefully meet, and the remaining chapters represent an attempt to enact serious conversations between these bodies. The issues covered are vast and wide-ranging. They emerged as preoccupying themes from a series of visits to intentional communities and are addressed by the bodies of thought.

Transgressive utopianism is oppositional, but in a particular sense. The book enacts a multiple conception of opposition in which many voices are directed at an issue. This, it is hoped, can begin to form an intellectual foundation for a politics of coalition. We see this occurring in practice as 'little old ladies' and crusty travellers stand together at road protests. People negotiate their differences and work together on single issues. The chapters that follow take a lead from this and add to this phenomenon the existing weight of the bodies of thought that are consulted.

Chapter 3 investigates the way in which theorists have approached the political. This chapter interrogates the convention of dividing the world into two spheres of thought and activity: public and private. Feminist contributions comprise the bedrock of this analysis and are applied to the lived reality of the ecological *oikos*, or household as found in intentional ecological communities. Intentional communities are places in which private things are politicised.

Examples are decisions regarding lifestyle: where to live, what to eat, how to dispose of your shit. Further, they are the 'private' homes of politicised individuals. The meeting of these utopian bodes facilitates a conceptual shift and 'the political', it is suggested, is contingent.

Chapter 4 is concerned to explore the concept of property and its attendants: ownership, work and value. Here the utopian canon is mined for insight. How do we justify owning things? Is property legitimate? Brief considerations of some of the most difficult and complex areas of political theory are undertaken here, and the lives and accounts of people who live in intentional communities are taken as accounts of an alternative approach to the concept of property. Further, I suggest that from the utopic spaces of the communities, we can engage in provocative theorisation of ownership, the relation between work and value, the role of money, self-worth and esteem. What happens, for instance, when work is detached from pay?

Chapter 5 is concerned to explore a recurrent theme of the book: relations of Self to Other. This, if you like, is the core theme of the book, though it cannot stand independently of the others. Our approach to the public and the private, our thinking on property and the accounts that we offer of Self and Other are all interconnected. Accounts of Self and Other explain how we think about ourselves in relation to others. The 'Other' in question may be another individual, or group of individuals, or a collective, or species. The accounts consulted in this chapter are drawn from deconstructive theory, psychoanalysis, social psychology, deep ecology, and from the New Age community of Findhorn. They all share a suspicion of account of Self and Other that sees us as in a state of perpetual opposition.

The approach taken in this book is at once flexible, fallible, modest, ambitious, pragmatic and principled. *Utopian Bodies* is, quite simply, an attempt at a new approach to thinking about theory.

1 Bodies of thought

Introduction

This chapter is about bodies of thought. It is my aim here to introduce the bodies to which the rest of the book refers. These are the sources of the theoretical base on which the subsequent chapters build. The sources are diverse and include the utopian canon, green political thought feminist thought and deconstructive theory. A central assumption of my methodology is the normative claim that different traditions of thought (genres, disciplines) can and, what is more, should learn from each other. Each involves its own rigours and training and each is protective of its identity and its particular truth claims. This is understandable, but the pursuit of knowledge, understanding or critique can become secondary to the protection of discipline. A certain amount of reflexivity is a positive thing: it enables us to be aware of our bias and our methods – and self-questioning is important, especially in those privileged to work in academe, which is sometimes believed to be a source of knowledge. However, disciplinary exclusivity sometimes requires recognition as self-serving and excessively introspective.

Discussions here are introductory and are structured to facilitate accessibility. The four areas under discussion are all very different. The aim is to comprehensibly introduce a range of fields in such a way as to adequately provide a feel for each. Each is considered in terms of their form, content and function. The utopian canon, for instance, is a body of thought by virtue of convention and generic association. In other words it is said to share a certain form, to be expressed in a certain shape, and to have certain identifiable conventions of content and function or purpose.

Each of the following sections will show why its subject can be said to constitute a body of thought. In the course of these discussions I shall elucidate the theory of transgressive utopianism upon which this book builds.

Utopian thought

Form

Utopias are invariably fictions. They imagine alternative realities; they stretch the conventions of the present; they re-present the world to us for inspection from another perspective; they imagine worlds transformed. As such they are an ideal place from whence to engage in political critique, and in which to explore alternative approaches to the world. The fact that they are fictive does not, however, mean that they are invariably articulated in the form of fiction. Utopias are expressed in a multitude of forms. Ernst Bloch identifies utopianism (a utopian impulse) as immanent in popular culture. His sources range from architecture to medicine; music to religion; art to philosophy (Bloch 1986). Most contemporary scholars of utopian thought accept that the field is broader than is often colloquially assumed, and include forms other than the novel in their research. For Vincent Geoghegan, the 'classic' utopia (the literary model established by Thomas More) is 'but one manifestation of utopianism' (Geoghegan 1987: 2). Ruth Levitas, in her thorough examination of the canon, finds the focus on literary form to issue an unnecessarily narrow definition (Levitas 1990: 4). Lyman Tower Sargent (1994), the major bibliographer of this field, has recently studied the utopias of the religious right in America as well as those of indigenous societies. This makes the study of utopianism a challenging process, which is potentially endless.

This inter-disciplinarity gives to utopian studies a special place in contemporary and historical traditions of scholarship. Research from even the narrowest approach to utopia – as a piece of fiction – involves cross-disciplinary work. A. L Morton's explorations of utopia exemplify this. He takes utopia as 'an imaginary country described in a work of fiction with the object of criticising existing society' (Morton 1952: 10). From this restricted definition, he studies works such as the fourteenth-century poem, *The Land of Cokaygne* and More's *Utopia* (1516). He refers to religious history, to politics and to economics in his discussion of these texts, and shows them to be engaged in critique of their contemporaneous societies. *The Land of Cokaygne* includes a commentary on the perceived crisis within the Christian church, involving anti-clericalism and theological debates. Both of these issues were, at the time, of political import. Themes of Thomas More's *Utopia* include discussions of the enclosure of common pasture (for intensive and profitable sheep farming), the role of counsel, the relation between monarch and pope, and the respective roles of state and church. These were debates of overbearing political import at the time of writing. In order to pay attention to the content of a given utopia, then, even a form-based approach has to engage in multi- or cross-disciplinary study of, in these cases, theology, politics and literature. Conversely, to pay attention simply to the content of a utopia (say, from the perspective of political science or philosophy) to the neglect of its form, is to study only one aspect of it. Form is important, as are factors of literary style, and attention to these things is necessary also. More's *Utopia*, for instance, cannot be appreciated without reference to the linguistic and etymological puns that partially veil so much of his satirical commentary. However, form is not a significant factor in identifying utopianism as such.

Content

The content of utopias has been subject to study from a wide range of perspectives. Some approaches are ideological. Examples are feminist and socialist approaches (given, for the sake of present argument, that feminism and socialism are ideologies). Others are specific to discipline, such as those from the fields of literary studies and political theory.

Discussions of content tend to take two forms. One focuses on formulaic content, the other looks for commonality of narrative content. The formulaic approach is exemplified in the work of J. C. Davies and Krishan Kumar. This approach typically aims to distinguish the utopia from other types of wish fulfilment. Utopias are said to be political, by which is meant 'institutional–bureaucratic' and to be concerned with organisational matters (Davis 1981). They are thought to be finite and perfectible and to offer a blueprint for the ideal polity (Davies 1981; Kumar 1991). I have argued against this approach to defining utopia on the grounds that its specifics are exclusionary of utopias that ought to be included in the genre (Sargisson 1996: 17–28). Examples are contemporary feminist utopias that broaden the conception of the political to include sexual relations (Wittig 1973) and child rearing (Carter 1982; Piercy 1979). An institutional–bureaucratic approach to politics is inadequate to this development. Further, this approach is inappropriate to texts that are unproblematically considered to belong to the canon. There is, for instance, a large body of secondary literature on More's *Utopia*, which suggests that it cannot be assumed to offer a straightforward blueprint for the perfect society. *Utopia* is subtle. 'Hythloday', the name given to the chief protagonist, means 'peddler of nonsense'; the word 'utopia' conflates two puns that combine as the 'good place that is no place'. The society of Utopia is not perfect: for instance, individual liberty is constrained by restrictions on speech and travel. Further, the puns and internal jokes in the text point to an attempt to do something other than sketch a vision of perfection.

Utopias, historically, have been shown frequently to contain certain formative conventions. One, I have said, is an attention to political critique (given the broadest sense of politics). Another is the visitor. Often an alien subject visits another world and views it from a position of critical estrangement (Kumar 1991). This figure is present in many utopias: Hythloday travels to the island of Utopia, William Guest visits another time in *News from Nowhere*, William Weston visits the land of Ecotopia (Callenbach 1975). The visitor may travel in space or time and is a useful protagonist. Utopias are also creative texts. They envisage alternatives, and offer spaces in which this is possible. They are playful and fun, often containing satirical wit. Attention to these conventions of form is useful when considering fictional utopias. However, care needs to be taken, as some of the assumed 'ingredients' have been mistakenly identified. For instance, utopias are not necessarily blueprints for the ideal world, though some may attempt this. An example is Francis Bacon's *New Atlantis* (1629). Nor do they necessarily evoke perfection, though, again, some may try to do this.

Bodies of thought 9

Definitions cast in terms of narrative content are unnecessarily exclusive. They are, I suggest, useful for identifying particular types of utopia: for instance, a green utopia might be expected to contain in its narrative some reference to a sustainable economy, respect for environment, and other cornerstones of ecological thought (Dobson 1995). Similarly, a feminist utopia might be characterised by its attention to women's role in society, and a critique of patriarchy (Pearson 1981: 63). The study of feminist and green utopias as such is a useful part of green and feminist speculation. However, attention to narrative content does not help us to distinguish utopias *per se*. Rather, this approach is divisive along lines of ideology or political bias. This kind of approach to the content of utopias is interesting and forms an essential part of their study, but does not enable us to identify them as a body of thought.

Utopias then have historically been diverse in terms of content, although certain conventions of formula can be said to constitute utopias as a genre of fictional writing. This rather tentative link is just one thing that connects them as a body of thought. In terms of narrative content they range widely. Plato's *Republic* has little in common in these terms with Marge Piercy's *Woman on the Edge of Time*. Both, however, are referred to in subsequent chapters as utopias. Both are approached as spaces in which certain utopian functions can be explored, and so it is to function that I shall now briefly turn.

Function

Some of the most interesting attempts to define utopianism as a body of thought focus on the area in which content and form combine to perform a particular function. The use of the visitor mentioned above, for instance, is a literary device often employed in fictional utopias. It provokes a certain sense of estrangement, which has a subversive political function. Utopias work from the margins of fantasy whilst addressing political desires and frustrations of the present. Krishan Kumar says that utopias are a particularly subversive form of political commentary, and notes that their authors have often experienced imprisonment and/or torture as political dissidents. He explains thus:

> Utopia challenges by supplying alternatives, certainly. It shows what could be. But its most persistent function, the real source of its subversiveness, is as a critical commentary on the arrangements of society.
>
> (Kumar 1991: 87–8)

As estranged texts, utopias are able to view from an imaginary distance the society whence they originate. They are, in this way, transgressive: they present a challenge to the *status quo*.

The creativity – and fictive nature – of much utopian writing also has a potentially transformative function. It forces interdisciplinary study on the part of the experts. It employs the novel as a vehicle for political critique. It presents theory

[handwritten margin notes: "Yet, they limit notions of utopianism – the impulse and affect of utopia."; "So, state two men say as Sargisse suggests"; "Again, use."; "CRITICAL UTOPIAS"]

as fiction, which is interesting. It creates a space in which philosophical ideas can be imagined, tested and explored. These are all specific functions that I have elsewhere linked in an approach to utopianism that stresses its transgressive function (Sargisson 1996). Briefly, I suggest, utopian thought is transgressive in three ways:

- it steps over boundaries that order and separate. Examples might be boundaries between disciplines, or conceptual boundaries, or boundaries that establish the norms of social behaviour.
- It thus renders them meaningless or emphasises their porosity.
- This permits the creation of a space where previously there was none, in which new and different ways of relating to the world can be practised.

These spaces are the new place that is no place: utopias.

Tom Moylan approaches utopia from a literary perspective. In *Demand the Impossible* (1986) he offers a conceptualisation of what he calls the critical utopia. This is a useful device. It stresses the dual function of utopian thought that, historically, has offered simultaneous political critique and the creation of something new. His understanding of utopia is informed by attention to form, content and function, the latter being the element that he stresses. Utopian thought, he finds, unsurprisingly, is rooted in discontent:

> It is, at heart, rooted in the unfulfilled needs and wants of specific classes, groups, and individuals in their unique historical contexts.
>
> (Moylan 1986: 1)

Its function is oppositional: utopia opposes 'the affirmative culture' (*ibid.*: 1):

> Utopia negates the contradictions of a social system by forging visions of what is not yet realised either in theory or in practice. In generating such figures of hope, utopia contributes to the open space of opposition.
>
> (*ibid.*: 1–2)

Unlike many commentators, who are concerned at the diversity and ambiguity of contemporary utopian writing, Moylan finds delight in this multiplicity. He sees it as historically specific and appropriate, and in my research on contemporary feminist utopianism I have built on this analysis. For Moylan, the multiple and diverse nature of recent utopias enables effective opposition to what he perceives as capitalist hegemony. These utopias, he says, are critical in two senses:

> 'Critical' in the Enlightenment sense of *critique* – that is expressions of oppositional thought, unveiling, debunking, of both the genre itself and the histori-

cal situation. As well as 'critical' in the nuclear sense of the *critical mass* required to make the necessary explosive reaction.

(Moylan 1986: 10)

In order to be effectively critical in these ways the utopia must, says Moylan, destroy, transform and revive the utopian tradition which, in its past and present state, was and is inadequate to the task of provoking social transformation. I have suggested, in *Contemporary Feminist Utopianism*, that it is not utopias themselves that have necessarily proved thus inadequate, but rather a mistaken reading of utopias as perfection-seeking, blueprinting and desirous of perfection and finality. For Moylan, a fixed, finite and universal utopia of perfection cannot adequately oppose a fixed, finite, and universal capitalist system. Only an understanding of utopia that destroys old perceptions of the genre, transforms them into something new and thus revives utopianism, can adequately reflect the concerns, needs and wants of contemporary malcontents. The critical utopia does not blueprint, but rather it privileges social change in process. It retains imperfection.

Moylan connects this critical utopianism to what he optimistically calls a 'new historic bloc' of political opposition (*ibid.*: 11). This, he says, consists of a historically specific collection of groups, linked by the source of their discontent. He finds the values of feminism, ecology and democratic socialism to infuse this bloc. These are manifested in an opposition to certain core values embodied in capitalist economy:

> Whatever the particular set up of social images each text sets forth, the shared quality in all of them is a rejection of hierarchy and domination and the celebration of emancipatory ways of being as well as the very possibility of utopian longing itself.
>
> (*ibid.*: 12)

I find this conception of utopia persuasive and appropriate certainly to contemporary feminist utopianism. Moylan's optimism regarding the unity of his bloc of opposition is excessive, but many of his arguments are borne out by my research into the contemporary (British) ecology movement. Opposition here is transformative in the way that he suggests, as well as being transgressive in the senses outlined above. This will be explored in the chapters that follow.

An important function of utopias then is that of transformative opposition. It is important to note that the multiple narratives, the disjointed texts, the stress on process that are common in many recent utopian novels are, in this reading, positive aspects of utopianism. They permit process to occur beyond the end of the text in question. They do not enforce closure. The import of this should become increasingly clear. For now, it is sufficient to note that the source of these utopian visions: feminism and ecologism, are not unified and cohesive bodies of thought (see pp. 12–25) and so an open-ended utopianism is particularly appropriate to them. Moylan over emphasises the unity of these movements. Such a move is unnecessary. A key theme of feminist thought today is the desire to maintain diversity and difference. Divisions within ecology movements, whether in theoretical terms of ecology and environmentalism, or in practical terms of the gradualism of the British Green Party compared without the radicalism of Earth First! leave this movement similarly fragmented. Nor can socialism be said to be unidirectional.

Summary

Utopian thought is expressed in a multitude of forms. Those focused on here are textual. Utopian theory and fiction contain a diverse range of political and ideological positions. As such, in terms of content, they do not form a cohesive whole. I have suggested, however, that utopianism comprises a body of thought for the following reasons.

- First, utopias are often expressions of an estranged perspective. Certain conventions within the body of fictional utopias enable form and style to enact this estrangement.
- Utopias express dissatisfaction with the political present. They are critical.
- Utopias are creative: they gesture towards alternative ways of living and being.
- They are subversive. They lead us to question the values and systems by which we are currently guided or governed.
- Utopias are significantly transgressive. This is in terms of style and form, and in the fact that they blend theory, political commentary and fiction. This is also in terms of their function which is, as I have said, to provoke us to think differently about the world. Hence,
- utopianism has a transformative function.

Different utopias will have different actual functions: Ernest Callenbach's green utopia *Ecotopia* has a different message to that contained in Monique Wittig's *The Lesbian Body*. The former is a straightforward expression of (a certain) green vision of an attainable and sustainable future (Callenbach 1975). The latter is more complex: an inscription of the female body from an altered perspective. Its aim is the creation of a new sense of female subjectivity (Wittig 1973). These two books are vehicles for different ideologies and have varying didactic and/or exploratory messages. The link, albeit tenuous, is that both create a utopian space for exploration. Within this space, the above functions can then be mobilised.

Green political thought

Form

Green political thought has as its sources the natural sciences, philosophy, religious and spiritual writing, political theory, fiction and poetry, and the visual arts. It is, at heart, interdisciplinary, and it finds expression in all of these forms. We cannot, then, take form as a factor that unites green thought as a body. Attention will be paid to form in the discussions that follow, though not as a defining characteristic.

Content

Secondary commentators identify a number of key elements that are said to characterise green political thought. This appears initially to be an unproblematic task. We might, for instance, intuit certain features to be central to green thought: a concern for the environment, for instance, and a consideration of the relationship of humanity to its environment. Once discussion moves beyond the banal, though, ambivalence becomes apparent regarding the coherence of green thought.

A division has been identified that has now become conventional between two types of green politics. The terms employed to describe these vary. Jonathan Porritt refers to shades of the same colour: light and dark green (Porritt 1984). Andrew Dobson prefers the terms environmentalist and ecologist (Dobson 1995). The split was originally noted by Arne Naess in the essay 'The shallow and the deep' (1973). For Naess, shallow ecology is focused on pollution and the depletion of resources. Its central objective, he says, is 'the health and affluence of people in the developed countries' (Naess 1973: 96). Deep ecology is more complex. It involves a shift in the way that we see the world. Naess describes this as 'Rejection of the man-in-environment image in favour of the relational, total-field image' (*ibid.*: 96). Further, egalitarianism is extended in deep ecology to embrace the entire biosphere – with the proviso that some killing and suppression and even exploitation may be necessary. Behind this latter idea is the commitment to an equal right for all things to 'live and blossom' (p. 96). Further components of deep ecology identified by Naess are a respect for principles of diversity and symbiosis, an anti-class posture to human life, the fight against the depletion of resources and against pollution, a commitment to the complexity of life, and finally, decentralised politics and local autonomy (*ibid.*: 96–100). Naess is sometimes referred to as the father of deep ecology, and his work is treated in this book as a primary source of this body of thought. Some commentators focus on what they see to be the defining characteristic of these two varieties of green politics. Tim O'Riordan stresses the different routes to change: technocentric and ecocentric (O'Riordan 1976). Robyn Eckersley looks to the roots of the respective analyses and terms them anthropocentric and ecocentric (Eckersley 1992). There is general agreement that these correspond to reformist and radical versions of green thought (Young 1993; Garner 1996).

The names applied, then, are many and various but, for current purposes, it is suffice to note that many commentators agree on the existence of a split between two types of green politics. This is determined by the content of these critiques. The one: shallow, light and reformist is concerned with environmental degradation and seeks to resolve this through the application of appropriate technology and economic policy. This is the 'technological fix' version of green politics in which catalytic converters and CFC-free aerosols represent paths to safe and responsible industry, consumption and leisure. The other: deep, dark, radical and ecocentric, is more complex and demands that we change our lives drastically. This green politics requires a shift in our consciousness of our place in the world. It seeks to change our political and economic systems and behaviour as well as to transform lifestyle, consumption and work – every aspect of daily life.

Most commentators regard these as two branches of the same ideology. This is apparent in the imagery of a spectrum of 'greenness', which correspond to a continuum of reformist to radical politics. For others though, these are two very different entities. Andrew Dobson's position would appear to suggest that to call green politics a 'body of thought' is to apply a misnomer. In *Green Political Thought*, Dobson is concerned to identify a 'set of ideas regarding the environment which can be properly regarded as an ideology' (Dobson 1995: 1). He draws a distinction between ecologism proper, in this sense, and environmentalism which is, he says, fundamentally different. The core component of environmental thought is, for Dobson, a 'managerial' approach to the environment. Environmentalists, as stated, believe in the efficacy of a technological fix to environmental crises. Correct consumption and production can, it is thought, redress current imbalances. He finds ecologism to be more thoroughgoing and complex: it issues deeper changes. It has a coherently mapped worldview, a prescriptive account of the good life and a plan for getting there. These latter form Dobson's criteria for an ideology. His separation of green thought in this way is not an act of pedantry, but rather addresses the status of both the ideology and any claims made in its name.

> the legitimacy of ideological prescriptions will be rooted in the kinds of observations to be found in works of political theory; they will not be thought through with the same rigour, but they will be there.
>
> (*ibid.*: 3)

If a statement is an ideological one, then, a theoretical base informs it. This may be unacknowledged. This gives to it a certain rigour and depth and it follows a certain legitimacy.

> to misunderstand the nature of green politics is to misconceive its historical significance as a challenge to the political, social, and scientific consensus that has dominated the last two or three hundred years of public life. Green politics self-consciously confronts dominant paradigms, and my task here is to ensure that it is not swallowed up by them and the interests that they serve.
>
> (*ibid.*: 7–8)

Dobson's separation of political ecologism from environmentalism serves intellectual rigour and political efficacy. To confuse the two, he says, is to confuse a thoroughgoing political critique which has a sound and thoughtful theoretical base, with a quick-fix superficial approach that does not challenge the dominant paradigms.

This challenge to the patterns of order and structure: paradigmatic challenge, is a feature of green thought that makes it an appropriate bed-partner for utopianism. Utopias also critique. They also map out the world and identify its imperfections. Further, obviously, they gesture towards the good life. They have a history of serving as vehicles of political theory. In terms of these functions, then, utopias behave as ideological tools. The content, of course, is variable. And they rarely offer a plan for their attainment. Only the blueprinting utopias do this at an explicit level. Others, I suggest, work more subtly by provoking us to think more carefully or differently about the world. They challenge things that we may take for granted by assuming an estranged viewpoint. In these ways, utopias also challenge paradigms. This is why I have elsewhere identified their key function as the permission of paradigm shifts in consciousness (Sargisson 1996).

For Dobson, then, ecologism and environmentalism are different, not in degree, but in kind. They are not different versions of the same ideology: they are rather different in their fundamentals. He acknowledges the need for flexible boundaries when creating theoretical categories, but says:

> This is right and proper – as long as we remember that we are not dealing with some ideological soup, and that as well as being sensitive to differences *within* ideologies, we must also retain a sense of the differences *between* them.
> (Dobson 1995: 4)

Environmentalism or shallow green politics is the property of the ideology that ecologism confronts. This, for Dobson, is why the separation is required. Not all commentators agree upon the value of a separation of green politics thus. John Barry, for instance, has suggested that the division does not serve the interests of political efficacy. The distinction of shallow from deep ecology, he says, distracts from the task of working out a rigorous position that is applicable to the political present (Barry 1994). This is a serious point, and the dangers of introspective scholarship have been mentioned above. Briefly, if a body of thought becomes the focus of study of-and-for-itself, there is a danger that it will gradually become detached from the 'real' empirically observable and experienced world that it pretends or aspires to study. However, if Dobson is correct, and there is a danger of absorption by the paradigms that it seeks to confront, then ecologism should certainly be held separate. Both of these positions have purchase.

I shall attempt to negotiate these demands of efficacy and rigour thus: the focus of my study is, on the one hand, the primary texts of deep ecology: the more utopian and thoroughgoing of the green positions. By studying it thus I hope to avoid any de-radicalisation of that body of thought. Further, it is generally agreed that this does represent a coherent (in the sense of clearly identifiable) body of thought. On the other hand though, and simultaneously, I shall explore the lived reality of green utopias: intentional communities. The accounts given by members of these communities, and my observations made whilst visiting them, will be taken as primary texts and sources of knowledge and information of green politics 'on the ground'. Any links that occur will be fortuitous and I shall attempt not to force these in my discussions.

Function

Green (deep) ecological politics aims to change the world. It is utopian in all senses of this word. It aims to achieve the impossible: its task is massive. It articulates political critique and the desire of malcontents. It aims to issue in a new way of being. It even occasionally blueprints the ideal polity. It is transgressive of dominant paradigms. It provokes shifts in the way that we think about ourselves. It may even be critical in Moylan's sense as it surely issues from an oppositional culture.

Green political thought is invariably apocalyptic. An intended function of green thought is the avoidance of ecological disaster. Catastrophic environmental analysis is taken as given. This was established by the work of natural and social scientists in the 1970s. Examples are James Lovelock's *Gaia Hypothesis* (1979) that established that the earth was a living organism, and the Limits to Growth thesis of the Club of Rome, which argued that current levels of resource depletion and consumption were unsustainable. These represent the empirical base of green concerns and inform shallow environmentalism as well as deep ecology. Deep ecologists are particular in their insistence that the only way to effectively confront imminent ecological disaster is to change the way that we think.

The paradigms confronted by deep ecology are thought to shape and form our thoughts. Put differently, they inform the way in which we are accustomed to think about ourselves. This is the subject of discussion in Chapter 5. All of the major primary texts take as their target what is called 'the western mindset'. Andrew Dobson nicely explains this:

> Central to the theoretical canon of green politics is the belief that our social, political, and economic problems are substantially caused by our intellectual relationship with the world and the practices that stem from it.
>
> (Dobson 1995: 39)

In particular, Dobson cites a habit of thinking that separates things: divides them and isolates them, rather than focusing on their connectivity and interdependence. Baconian and Newtonian science, Cartesian philosophy and Christian theology are frequently mentioned in the texts as contributors to this worldview. Here, 'man' dominates the natural world by right and by virtue of his ability to do so. This is an anthropocentric approach. This view is attributed to post-Enlightenment science and philosophy: the world can be fully comprehended, if it is studied sufficiently closely. Conversely, Greens believe themselves to be in the company of the leading edge of contemporary science when they insist instead upon a 'systems view' (Dobson: 41; Mathews

1991). This science does not see the world as hierarchically arranged or structured by opposition. Rather it insists that one area is connected to and dependent on another. Knowledge is contingent and always incomplete.

For some, this means that green political thought requires attention to our inner natures or spirits. Here the voice of Rudolf Bahro is perhaps the most insistent. In *Avoiding Social and Political Disaster* (1994), Bahro characteristically identifies a spiritually deficient mindset as real source of the world's problems.

> In view of the intention to combine spirituality and politics, my book has two interwoven strands, an inner and an outer line of approach to the problems of a Turn-around movement.
>
> (Bahro 1994: 12) The Mega Machine.

Of course, he says, pollution, environmental degradation and socially unacceptable behaviour are also problems. But these are symptomatic of a mass psychosis (he does not use this term) which ground the 'megamachine'. This is why the 'inner' and more difficult line of the book is, he says, the decisive one. The megamachine is the infrastructure that is in-built in contemporary Western capitalist societies. We are all complicit in it. Its (and our) basic goals are 'more, faster, and bigger' (Bahro 1994: 1). We need to stop the megamachine and dismantle it: only then can we build something new. The scope of the change demanded by Bahro is vast. The social mores that comprise the megamachine are, he says, inside our souls. They comprise what he calls the logic of self-annihilation. Only once a critical mass of the population has accomplished a significant shift in the way they think can sustainable change be established. This, he says, takes us in the direction of a logic of salvation. Underlying political and economic problems, then, are problems of psychology.

In addition to the substance of his analysis, Bahro's significance is in his demands on political philosophy. The green and peace movements, he says, require help. They cannot achieve this shift in consciousness without a theory that takes into account their spiritual needs. His aim is to add to green politics some spiritual depth:

> Meanwhile there is nothing more important than to expand and deepen the mental and spiritual bases of the ecological and peace movement.
>
> (*ibid.*: 10)

This calls for a new kind of politics: one that is not closed to spirituality. Further, it speaks to the way in which we should study politics and the environment. It forces interdisciplinary study and resists the closure and certainty of some approaches. Partiality and process become as important as answers and solutions. Robyn Eckersley suggests this, and it is a belief that is consistently asserted in my own work (Eckersley 1992; Sargisson 1996). The approach taken will, of course, impact upon the outcome of research. This much is obvious. Methodologically though, the desires and aspirations of the researcher should be owned without opacity. This research seeks to explore the utopian confrontation of paradigms without establishing a re-assertion of those paradigms. If green utopian bodies challenge them, then it is not my desire to re-affirm them by seeking tidy conclusions or neat answers.

This is a far-reaching aspect of deep ecology, which issues from that body's affinity for fundamentalist (Bahro 1994) or holistic (Kemp and Wall 1990) approaches to theory. This assumes the most effective way of approaching a problem to be to go for its roots. The form and function of theory thus produced tends to be complex and to stress connections rather than separate entities. This further confronts the paradigms identified by green thinkers as contributory factors to human, environmental and planetary degradation.

One further element of green thought, which is said to contribute to its opposi-tional and critical function, is the special role assigned to 'the feminine'. Green thinkers often cite patriarchy, or masculinity, as a source of a separating and hierarchical consciousness. At the level of activism, Penny Kemp and Derek Wall state that 'The Green movement is very much a women's movement'. They proceed to cite the work of feminists, such as Susan Griffin, who attribute to women and the environment a shared source of oppression: patriarchy (Kemp and Wall 1990: 18–19). Rudolf Bahro describes patriarchy as a 'fundamental mode of consciousness' (Bahro 1994: 134). It incites a 'will-to-mastery' (p. 125), and is thus connected to the logic of self-extermination:

> It is clear that, excluding mere exchange, 'war', 'commerce' and 'piracy', money and capital, state and church, rationalistic science and technology are wholly masculine inventions and institutions. The existence of Amazons, female hustlers, queens, female saints or women like Marie Curie, cannot refute this. The roles are written out and distributed in advance, and women are allowed to play along. But the spirit and the methods are essentially masculine, and women modulate things only a little.
>
> (Bahro 1994: 121)

An attention to so-called feminine characteristics is thought by some (including Bahro) to redress a fundamental imbalance in the Western psyche, which has been dominated by masculine drives for achievement and acquisition for so long that these things appear 'human nature'. This is just one way in which patriarchy is thought to oppress both women and the non-human world. I shall pursue these points further below. For now it is sufficient to note a claimed affinity between women and nature: deep ecology and feminism (or femininity).

Summary

Deep ecology is a body of thought for the following reasons. It contains shared themes and concerns, which combine to a particular function:

- An attention to the fundamentals of the relationship between humans and their context or environment, and an attempt to re-develop our understandings of this relation.
- A desire for the redress of perceived imbalances in the distribution of value: feminine and masculine, human and non-human. Ecocentrism, which is discussed further in Chapter 5, aims to shift the focus of thought completely from the human sphere to that of life *per se*.
- A holistic approach to problem solving. It aims at the root of problems, and is not concerned merely to tinker with superficial manifestations of those issues.
- A strong spiritual element.
- And, centrally, at the heart of deep green thought, is a utopian and ambitious aim: to change the way that we think. Everything above is aimed at this transformative function: to oppose and transgress the paradigms that currently limit and restrict our thinking. Only this, they explicitly assert, can ground sustainable political change.

Feminist political thought

Form

Feminist thought finds expression in multifarious forms and so form cannot be used to identify this as a body of thought. Feminist thought is explored in, for instance, film, literature: novels and poetry, science, medicine, philosophy, works of visual art – the list goes on and on. Feminist thought is articulated outside and inside academe and, increasingly, attempts are made to establish resonance between these different voices. There is, within feminist movements, a history of deliberate avoidance of established media of expressing political thought. This stems in part from a radical feminist rejection of masculine vehicles of expression and change. The disciplines, as with the institutions, are thought to be thoroughly and fundamentally patriarchal and feminist scholars find themselves drowning in the 'malestream' of objective scholarship and methodologies, which render them impotent in the name of rigour:

> Indeed, the texts of phallocratic ethicists function in the same manner as pornography, legitimating the institutions which degrade women's be-ing.
>
> (Daly 1979: 13)

> In scientific research, it is rarely admitted that data have been gathered and interpreted from a particular perspective. Since scientific research centres on the physical and natural worlds, it is presumed 'objective'; therefore, the term perspective does not apply to it.
>
> (Rosser 1993: 253)

The ideal of normative reason, moral sense, stands opposed to desire and affectivity. Impartial civilised reason characterises the virtue of the republican man who rises above passion and desire. . . . Insistence on the ideal of impartiality in the face of its impossibility functions to mask the inevitable partiality of perspective from which moral deliberation actually takes place.

(Young 1986: 23)

These statements come from a sample of fields: theological philosophy, medical ethics and political science. Simply put: feminist female scholars have found it hard to find and make heard their voices in the context of academic research. This is thought to be due in large part to the culture and paradigms that govern these areas. For this reason the study of feminist thought is both inter- and anti-disciplinary, and involves the consideration of academic and popular sources. Reference will be made in subsequent chapters to works from a range of sources that include philosophy, psychoanalysis, fiction and political theory. Special attention will be paid to the utopias found in these areas, be they fully articulated utopian visions or moments of utopic imagining and creativity.

Content

In terms of content, feminism is diverse and varied and even, in some readings, self-contradictory. I say 'in some readings' by way of qualification: some approaches to feminism result in a picture of that movement as incoherent and internally flawed. One way of seeking to identify a body of thought is to characterise it in terms of ideological content. This approach specifies an ideal type, and names features that comprise a particular ideology. This is not dissimilar to the approach taken by Andrew Dobson to green political thought, which is outlined above. Taking this approach to feminist thought allows us neatly to pigeonhole it into such categories as 'liberal feminism', 'socialist feminism' and 'radical feminism'.

This is a popular way into the morass that is feminist thought and is often assumed in introductory textbooks (Jagger 1983; Bryson 1992). It has pedagogical and heuristic value, but is artificially divisive. It allows us to see that within feminist thought there are indeed maps to the political world, visions of the good life and plans about how to get there (Dobson's criteria for an ideology). Also it permits us to note that there are several competing versions of each of these. Feminism, then, appears not to be a single ideology and is thus, in some way, a failure. It had become commonplace in introductory discussions to consider feminism thus – in terms of its 'branches'. These are the creation of political theorists and are tools of convenience. I shall use the terms 'liberal', 'radical', 'black', 'post-structuralist', etc. as descriptive terms in subsequent chapters, but have reservations about the definitive value of this approach.

A few words are perhaps necessary about one 'branch' of feminist thought that appears particularly appropriate to this study – ecofeminism. Ecofeminism attempts a union of ecologism and a certain kind of feminism, which has its origins in radical feminism. There are, within ecofeminism, trends leading in two broad directions. Both see women and the non-human environment to share a source of oppression, which is masculine. One insists (following radical feminism) that men and women are essentially and fundamentally different and that women have the answers to planetary degradation. This view stresses a positive role for 'the feminine'. Characteristics that are the property of women are valorised. Examples are compassion and spirituality (Metzger 1989), an intimate relation with the body (Spretnak 1989) and nurture (Merchant 1990). The other trend shares certain features with post-structuralism and takes what is claimed to be a non-essentialist (metaphysical?) approach to sex and gender differences. In this reading, epitomised in the work of Mary Mellor and Val Plumwood, masculinity and femininity are part of a dualistic and hierarchical paradigm that forms the underlay for the way that Western political philosophy and science approach the world. In these accounts masculinity and femininity are viewed as artificial constructs that historically coincide with men and women but that are not thus forever after. It is not, in other words, inexorably linked to biological sex. The latter is more sophisticated and appropriate to twentieth-century contexts than is the former. A feminism that accepts essential differences between (biological) men and women and then proceeds to invert the hierarchical domination of the one over the other is, as its critics suggest, regressive and naïve (Biehl 1991; 1993).

It may be that ecofeminism bears a special relation to deep ecology and to green politics, but it will not be the only 'type' of feminism consulted here. Ecofeminism is not the only point at which feminism and ecologism touch. Historically, much feminist thought refers to connections between women and 'nature'. Often, technology has been viewed as a route to the emancipation from biological and social inequality. For some, technology is a vehicle for planetary transformation. Shulamith Firestone, writing in 1971, attempted to place a Marxist framework onto feminist thought. Part of her hope for feminist revolution lay in escaping the institution of the nuclear family – a source of oppressive socialisation. She calls for a revolutionary ecological programme that will free women from their biology:

> A revolutionary ecological programme would ... establish an artificial (man-made) balance in place of the 'natural' one, thus realizing the original goal of empirical science: total mastery of nature.
>
> Nature provided a fundamental inequality – half the human race must bear and rear the children of all of them – which was later consolidated, institutionalized, in the interests of men.
>
> (Firestone 1971: 217, 222)

She seeks from technology extra-uterine gestation. Only thus, she suggests, can the link between biology and social destiny be broken. There is little in this approach to commend itself to deep ecology or to most contemporary green thought. However, Marge Piercy's *Woman on the Edge of Time*, which is to an extent a fictional enactment of Firestone's utopia, is often referred to as an ecological utopia. Like Firestone, Piercy envisages a technological disruption of women's 'natural' functions:

> It was part of the women's long revolution. When we were breaking all the old hierarchies. Finally there was one thing we had to give up too, the only power we ever had, in return for no more power for anyone. The original production: the power to give birth. Cause as long as we were biologically enchained, we'd never be equal.
>
> (Piercy 1979: 105)

Piercy's fictional utopia contains many themes that might designate it ecological and feminist. Relations between humans and their environment are egalitarian and politically inclusive, and a paradigm of ecological consciousness is in operation. Her attitude towards technology though is markedly different to the organic, dualistic, naturalist form of feminism that has become known as ecofeminism. I shall consult this utopia for the ideas it explores that touch upon themes of this book and not simply because it is sometimes described as ecofeminist. Questions of inclusion and exclusion are decided upon on these rather pragmatic grounds throughout this book. Ecofeminism *per se* gets special treatment here only. I am actually wary of feminisms of inversion and find them to be of limited value. Other areas of feminist thought though have been neglected by ecologism and will be drawn upon. Examples are feminist contributions to the conceptualisation of 'the political', which is dealt with in Chapter 3.

An alternative to the 'branches' approach to the content of feminism is one that characterises it as a body of thought that consists of chronological periods or 'waves'. These are normally taken to be 'first wave' feminism: from 1830 to 1920, and 'second wave feminism' from the 1960s to the current day. The first wave assumed a campaign for liberal universal rights, and the second argues that women and men were significantly different beings. Some commentators speak also of a 'third wave', which focuses on the differences amongst women (Plumwood 1993b). This approach presents feminism as a continuum: growing, changing, developing and evolving. Its danger though is that it tends to neglect to pay sufficient attention to the diversity that has always existed in feminist thought. This is brought most effectively to our attention by black feminists such as bell hooks (1984) and Patricia Hill Collins (1991). These writers suggest to feminism that it has always been at best exclusive and at worst imperialistic as a movement. It has always been the property of women who have the luxury of whiteness and its accompanying privileges of power and access.

Increasingly, feminist thought is accepted for its diversity of content and some commentators pluralise the word 'feminism' to indicate this. The excellent reader *Feminisms* from Sandra Kemp and Judith Squires accompanies this pluralistic device with a deliberate resistance to a project of definition (1997). Definitions are thought to be totalising and repressive of difference and to misrepresent the reality of feminist thought and activity. This book also takes an approach that attempts to combine rigour with ethical representation. Feminism is taken by Kemp and Squires to be a body of critical analysis:

> Feminist theory might then be best characterised as critical analysis of the dynamics of gender and sexuality.
>
> (Kemp and Squires 1997: 6)

Such an approach does not shy away from the real differences (ontological, epistemological, ideological and political) that exist in feminist thought. Neither does it view this multiplicity as some kind of failed coherence:

> Whether the fragmentation, institutionalisation, and culturization of feminism are perceived as the sorry demise and de-radicalism of feminism, or as the maturation of increasingly flexible, self-reflexive, and multiple feminisms, one thing is evident: there is no unchanging feminist orthodoxy, no settled feminist conventions, no static feminist analyses. Feminism is diverse and it is dynamic.
>
> (*ibid.*: 12)

Certain themes and issues occupy contemporary feminist thought, which can be loosely characterised. These revolve increasingly around questions of identity (individual and group). They involve attention to academe and its paradigms, which are rigorously confronted. If the world of academic study is to be a vehicle to understanding or the asking of pertinent questions, then it requires that the tools of study be appropriate to these tasks. Further, individual identity and conceptions of Self preoccupy many feminists. This occurs in the fields of psychology, psychoanalysis and linguistics – in which attempts at reconceptualising gendered identity are made, as well as in political theory, film and the study of visual art. Women's identity as a 'group' is also the focus of these areas, as well as in cultural studies and, of course, women's studies. Other, related, preoccupying themes are the aims of feminist politics: equality or difference, and how best to get there once goals have been established.

Feminism is, I suggest, a body of thought that can be loosely understood in terms of content. A more thoroughgoing analysis requires attention also to function.

Function

Feminist work in academe seeks to submit to rigorous scrutiny that which it finds exclusive or oppressive. Often this involves interrogation of the foundations and methods of enquiry. Often, in other words, feminism submits academic disciplines to internal scrutiny. This means exploring and identifying paradigms that inform and form research. Outside of the academy too, feminist thinkers and actors are challenging and undermining many of the ways in which we think about the world. This, I suggest, is the core function of feminist thought: challenging assumptions and changing the way that we think. This is apparent, for instance, in the extracts cited on pp. 19–20, which were offered as examples of how broad-ranging critique is undertaken from within academic disciplines. Each of those quotations involves reference to a paradigm:

> Indeed, the texts of phallocratic ethicists function in the same manner as pornography, legitimating the institutions which degrade women's be-ing.
>
> (Daly 1979: 13)

Here, Mary Daly refers to the tradition of objective scholarship that, from her perspective, devalues the feminine. It does this through a process of intellectual legitimisation of gender exclusion. She seeks an inverted hierarchy in which women can (are permitted and given space in which to) be.

> In scientific research, it is rarely admitted that data have been gathered and interpreted from a particular perspective. Since scientific research centres on the physical and natural worlds, it is presumed 'objective'; therefore, the term perspective does not apply to it.
>
> (Rosser 1993: 253)

Sue Rosser argues that objective science is blind to its own gender bias.

> The ideal of normative reason, moral sense, stands opposed to desire and affectivity. Impartial civilised reason characterises the virtue of the republican man who rises above passion and desire. ... Insistence on the ideal of impartiality in the face of its impossibility functions to mask the inevitable partiality of perspective from which moral deliberation actually takes place.
>
> (Young 1986: 23)

Iris Marion Young's essay is, similarly, suggesting that the paradigms that organise research have a cultural and historical association with masculinity.

These women come from different feminist perspectives: their goals are different, but all identify *a way of thinking* to be at the root of gender inequality. Their desires lead in different directions, but are similar in nature: all seek to undermine and in some way change the way that we approach research (and thus, the world). This is a utopian desire: it is far-fetched, and it is estranged (women are excluded because they fail to possess the 'appropriate' characteristics). It expresses dissatisfaction, and it aims at subversion and transformation. In all of these ways it aims at a significantly transgressive function. Not only does feminism speak to similar themes and issues as ecologism then; it shares utopian potential as a body of thought.

Not all feminist theory issues a politics that is significantly different to the *status quo*. Ecofeminism and early radical feminism, for instance, tend to stop at the point of inversion without significantly changing the oppositional paradigm itself.[1] In other words, they retain a notion of opposition and domination in their utopias (with women on top, this time). However, these forms of feminism are nonetheless utopian in their aims. They seek to create new conceptual space, in which the world can be re-appraised:

> Ecological thinking and practice demands the highest consciousness and requires that each of us change the essential patterns of our life which are based more upon exclusivity, distinction, and elimination, separation, than upon inclusivity, unification, and relationship.
>
> (Metzger 1989: 121)

I mention this by way of acknowledging that utopian thought is not unproblematic. It does facilitate the creation of conceptual and physical spaces in which significantly transgressive and politically transformative thought and practice can occur. We might not, however, be happy with the content of these spaces.

Summary

Feminism constitutes a body of thought not in its form or because it contains a single ideology, but because it has the following functions:

- It is concerned with a critical assessment of the role of women in society. Contemporary feminism is particularly concerned with issues of power and identity.
- It aims to change the way that 'we' (men and women) think about the world. This applies to all areas of research and life; for example, history, politics, science, philosophy, culture and everyday life. This is attempted by subverting the paradigms of research as well as through the media of film and fiction.
- It aims to change the *status quo* of gendered reality. Feminism is diverse and even diffuse, being marked by plurality – the nature of the desired change may then vary, but the desire for change *per se* is constant.
- It has utopian potential. It is rooted in dissatisfaction with the present. It comes from an estranged (alienated) perspective and, as such, it creates spaces in which we can think differently about the world.

Deconstructive thought

Form

Deconstructive thought has its roots in post-structuralist analyses of power

---

1 I do not refer here to the 'deconstructive' work of Plumwood and Mellor.

and language. As such, it has a historical link to a number of forms of expression. These are textual and academic and are concerned, broadly, with literature and politics. This approach has its roots in literary study and in particular in the study of language. Also it is connected – loosely – with so-called 'post-modernism'. This latter finds expression in a range of fields, from film, sculpture and visual arts, music and fiction, to philosophy, science and political theory. Because deconstruction has roots in the study of language, it involves a technical vocabulary that is, at first glance, quite alienating and that are peculiar to this form. Often people are put off by this. However, this body of thought is sufficiently useful to both feminist politics and green politics to make the task of approaching deconstructive jargon worth the effort.

Content and function

I have chosen to refer to this body of thought as deconstructive rather than post-modern or post-structuralist because my use of this body of thought in this book is highly selective. For me, it is identifiable by reference to content and function which are, in this case, inseparable. Deconstructive thought contains a number of recurring themes. These include, first, an attention to language and its relation to reality and, subsequently, analysis of the ways in which we are accustomed to think about the world. It has utopian potential, and contains moments of utopian creativity (Sargisson 1996: 64–98). As such, it is of value to the current discussion.

Like deep ecologism and like much feminist thought, deconstructive thought identifies amorphous and complex sources to current political exclusions and inequalities. These are elusive. Power, following Nietzsche and Foucault, is shown to be diffusely located and self-perpetuating. It is thought to operate in structures of language. That is to say, in the structures by which we make sense of the world and communicate this to others. It is thought also to operate in the rules and codes that govern our relationships with others: other individuals and other groups of people and non-humans. Often, this approach is condemned as wilfully opaque, pretentious and unnecessarily difficult. However, this is not necessarily the case. If the sources of exclusions that cause political discontent are complex, then accounts of this are bound to be complicated.

Deconstruction, in this book, is used as a way of reading. What is read though is more than just printed texts. If language informs politics and is part of political exclusion, as post-structuralists suggest, then language is part of the problem. This has two immediate implications. First, and most apparently, it tends to produce accounts that are self-consciously opaque. This is because, evidently, if language is part of the problem, then it forms a vehicle of ambiguous transformative value:

> If we continue to speak the same language to each other, we will reproduce the same story.
>
> (Irigaray 1980: 67)

Second, language itself is treated in deconstructive approaches as a text. Language is thought to 'write' certain codes and patterns of association into our communication with others. It inscribes our culture. This lies behind Jacques Derrida's oft-cited statement that there is nothing outside the text. These codes and paradigms are thought to be dualistic and oppositional. Meaning, in other words, is constructed through opposition. Sense is made of a concept by reference to its opposite. Goodness, for example, is contrasted to badness. Further, it is held that this is hierarchical and that it forms a system.

This might, for instance, account for the way in which nature is referred to by contrast to culture or humanity. The human sphere has been historically separated from and privileged over the natural sphere. Humans dominate nature. We use the 'natural' world to our own ends. This is legitimised by reference to a cluster of concepts. Humans said to be in possession of a number of properties that, it is assumed, put us rightfully in charge. These include the potential for rational thought and action, and can be schematically represented thus:

Human	Non-human
Culture	Nature
Rational	Instinctive

Deconstructive thought aims to show that 'humanity' and 'nature' are constructs (Simmons 1993). It attempts to unravel cultural and linguistic associations and constructions. Deconstruction is deliberately transgressive. It works by breaking the rules of association and structure that inform language and it thus permits new ways of looking at the world. For this reason, I have suggested it is utopian. Key terms in deconstructive accounts are those highlighted above: opposition, dualism, hierarchy and systems of meaning. Common points of reference are property and relations of Self and Other, and this body of thought is consulted in the chapters on these topics.

Feminism and deconstructive thought are increasingly linked in contemporary feminist theory. This is particularly the case in French feminism. There is, however, a very limited amount of crossover between feminism, ecologism and deconstruction. This is most apparent in the work of Mary Mellor and Val Plumwood. This book aims to contribute to this, and to suggest that a plurality of approaches is both useful and ethical.

Summary

Deconstruction has its roots in literary studies and draws much of its vocabulary from this source. It usually appears in a theoretical form. It is characterisable by reference to content and function:

- It interprets the relationship between language and power.

- It expresses a belief that language is dualistic, oppositional and hierarchical in structure.
- It is focused on a number of recurring themes. Examples are property, gender and relations of Self to Other.
- It has utopian potential.
- It is significantly transgressive of form (it is anti-disciplinary), content (internal transgression of the codes and structure of language) and function (it permits paradigmatic shifts in consciousness).

Conclusion

Feminism, green politics (and deep ecologism in particular) and deconstructive thought blend together in this book, yet attempts are made to retain a sense of their distinctness as bodies of thought. The boundaries are porous: ecologism spills into feminism, and parts of both are touched by deconstructive thought. It is not my desire to dissolve them: to assimilate them and take away their differences, yet I think that interesting and politically useful things happen when they meet.

From the synthesis or meeting of these bodies there issues a theorising that attempts to permit many voices to be heard. These are focused on the themes of this book. These themes in turn are the prodigy of my visits to bodies of people who are living in intentional communities that in some way connect to environmental politics. It is my contention that this route to thinking about theory, which draws on the accounts and experiences and observations of lived reality, as well as on a range of related, but distinct, bodies of thought is of interest and value. It permits us to transcend disciplinary expectations and limitations, and to look through the eyes of many concerned parties, at difficult and pressing issues of contemporary political life.

2 Bodies of people

Wherever the will to develop a new lifestyle arises, there is a way forward.

(Rudolf Bahro 1994: 3)

Introduction

Intentional communities are bodies of people who have chosen to live – and usually work in some way – together. They have a common aim or commitment. This commitment might be to such things as a political ideology, a spiritual path or to co-operative living itself. Those studied in the course of research for this book are self-described as environmentalist. Intentional communities are sometimes referred to as 'utopias'. One aim of this chapter is to clarify the sense in which these communites are characterised in this book as utopian bodies.

Utopianism is often given as a negative or derogatory description to evoke something excessively idealistic or impractical. The communities described below are real, working entities. Some are struggling and all experience difficult times. Communities sometimes fail. Nonetheless, new ones start up, old ones are revived or refreshed, and the oldest included here has been growing since its inception in 1962. The visions and aims of intentional communities are often ambitious and might be described as utopian in this negative sense, but often they are realised, nonetheless. Members of these communities have commitment and energy and are active political agents. They are not, then, communities of unpractical dreamers, escaping from the harsh realities of life. Life in each of the communities visited is, in its own way, challenging, and most people's motivations for living in community are political, ideological and/or spiritual.

Fictional and theoretical utopias are sometimes described as 'blueprints for perfection'. I have argued, in the chapter above, that this term is mistakenly applied. Often textual utopias gesture towards alternatives, but few attempt to design the perfect world. Intentional communities certainly do not make claims to perfection. Members are often excessively critical of their community. Nonetheless, they do see themselves as playing a transformative role and welcome interested visitors – they aim, in this way, to demonstrate the viability of alternative lifestyles.

Political utopianism in works of theory and fiction is invariably critical. They offer a critique of their own reality. The members of intentional communities all express dissatisfaction with the political and social *status quo*. Tom Moylan has suggested that literary utopias are critical also in a nuclear sense in that they contribute to a critical mass of opposition (Moylan 1986). One aim of this chapter is to begin to ask whether this applies also to the lived utopian bodies that are intentional communities.

Another hallmark of a textual utopia is its creativity. Fictional and theoretical utopias are imaginative. They have the scope and freedom to stretch and challenge conventional boundaries of the possible, the likely and the conceivable. Intentional communities are spaces in which similar things can occur. This is touched upon in the brief introductions below. It is explored more thoroughly in the chapters that follow.

Method

Each of the following communities was visited at least once. A combination of research methods was applied. For further details see Appendix B. Briefly, these comprised participant observation, semi-structured qualitative interviews and a quantitative survey.

Participant observation is a long-established method of anthropological research, in which the researcher lives, works and plays alongside the society or community that is the object of study (see, e.g., Jorgenson 1989). Extensive fieldnotes are taken, which are faithfully consulted afterwards. This method allows researchers to see and feel the situation for themselves. It does not presume an objective approach and personal bias and opinion is acknowledged as such.

Extended interviews have a number of functions. The researcher uses an interview schedule, which consists of the same questions – all of which are put to each volunteer. A copy of this is included in Appendix B. Some of the questions asked were broad in scope, so as to permit the interviewee to tell as much or as little as they felt appropriate (Foddy 1994). This yielded interesting material for analysis. For instance, it is significant that in most cases the question 'Could you describe this community for me?' yielded in 50 per cent of cases a physical description of the location, and in 50 per cent an account of the people. At communities associated with the Findhorn Foundation, however, everyone began with an account of the people. This is indicative of the ethos of that community. Within this method, there is also scope for asking supplementary questions. This permits flexibility and the pursuit of material and topics in greater depth (Holstein 1995). These interviews generally lasted between 1 and 3 hours.

I only interviewed volunteers. In some communities this meant that I spoke to everyone, but this was not always the case. The statements and testimonies are, with one exception (Chapter 5), taken as personal accounts and not as samples or representative statements of the community. Clearly, the views of individuals contribute towards the culture (political and otherwise) of a given community, but my concern in gathering this material was not to seek quantifiably representative samples (otherwise I would have rigidly interviewed a percentage of each community.) I wanted to permit flexibility, to allow for voluntarism and to focus on personal accounts.

The communities

The Findhorn Foundation

The Findhorn Foundation is an umbrella organisation under whose auspices are several intentional communities and a myriad of satellite associations and businesses. Most of these have charitable status. The Foundation takes its name after the village of Findhorn, on the East Coast of Scotland, in Morayshire. There are two core elements to all Findhorn Foundation enterprises and communities: spirituality and education. They combine to inform one of the major centres of New Age teaching and learning. This is self-described in the following terms:

> It [the Foundation] was founded in 1962 by Eileen and Peter Caddy and Dorothy Maclean on the principles that God, or the source of life, is accessible to each of us at all times, and that nature, including the planet, has intelligence and is part of a much larger plan.
> (Coates *et al.*, *Diggers and Dreamers* 1996/7: 119)

Findhorn has an international constituency and world-wide influence.

The discussions below are focused on the communities I visited. I shall also include reference to associated enterprises. The communities are based on two sides of northern Scotland. The community loosely referred to as 'Findhorn' or 'The Findhorn Foundation Community' is in two sites on the East Coast. The community of Erraid is on the West Coast.

Findhorn: Cluny and The Park

Physical space

Cluny Hill College is a huge and grand former hotel, in beautiful gardens, overlooking a golf course. This is the main centre for housing guests and students. Guest rooms are large and mostly shared. Staff members have their own rooms. Communal space inside the College includes a large and spacious dining room where guests and members eat together, a ballroom – which is used for dancing and as a space for workshops, and a sanctuary.

The Park has a different atmosphere to Cluny. Cluny is weighty and intense, though not unpleasantly so. The Park is light and more effervescent. There are a greater variety of buildings here and this is where the Foundation started in

1962. It comprises caravans (mobile homes and smaller touring vans), chalets of various types and eco-buildings. The vans are part of the Foundation's history as it was in one of these that the three founders initially lived with their children. There is, however, an ongoing programme of replacement and the desire is to establish the community in sustainable ecological housing. To this end there is a variety of buildings. Older ones are of the prefabricated kind, and some look like beach huts. The oldest permanent structure is The Nature Sanctuary: a stone-built mediation sanctuary. Newer buildings are made from recycled materials incorporating some of the latest ideas and technology in green building (Talbott 1997). The more picturesque of these are the 'whiskey-barrel houses'. These are large round wooden homes made of large timber vats from a local distillery. In another area is a group of about twenty two-storey buildings, made of wood. There are also a number of single-storey wooden chalets with steel-lined turf-covered roofs, which apparently weigh 7 tonnes. The Park also has its own (75 kW) windmill, the energy from which goes to the National Grid. Most of these structures were built in the 1980s.

The Community Centre is at the heart of The Park. This building contains spaces that are used for meetings as well as the kitchen and dining room, where guests and members eat together. The Universal Hall, a grand stone-built structure, houses large events like conferences and dances, as well as a visitor's centre. The cafe is open to the visiting public, as is the Phoenix Shop.

The most recent building programme involves an area that was a poppy-filled field at the time of my first visit in the summer of 1997. This is called 'The Field of Dreams' and plots were then on sale to people who had some connection with the community (Open Community members – staff are unlikely to have the funds, of which, more below). An eco-village is planned for this site. It is self-defined in terms not incompatible with deep ecology:

> As we define it, an Ecological Village is a human settlement that is sustainable ecologically, economically, culturally and spiritually; that expresses our essential relationship and connection to spirit and nature through its forms and structures.
>
> (Ecovillage website: http://www.findhorn.org/ecovil, 7 January 1999)

Experimentation has occurred with straw-bale structures but some difficulty has been encountered with gaining planning permission for these as dwellings. There is, consequently, a very fine shed.

One of the most innovative ecological structures is The Living Machine. It was opened in October 1996. It is an anaerobic sewage disposal system, with a difference.

> In a Living Machine, waste water is pumped to large underground holding tanks that serve as anaerobic reactors where much of the solid matter is digested. The stream then moves through a series of open tanks that each have a unique ecosystem of microorganisms and plants which break down

wastes and absorb them as nutrients. At the midpoint suspended solids are collected and recycled into the anaerobic reactors. Finally a set of tanks called 'ecological fluidised beds' filled with local and exotic aquatic plants and animals complete the cycle with final polishing. After that the water is ready for garden use or discharge into the local watercourse.

(Conference proceedings, *Eco-Villages and Sustainable Communities* 1997: 63)

By the time the sewage reaches the end tank it is extremely high quality water. The organic material has been reduced; the toxic ammonia has been changed into nitrogen gas; any metals present have been sequestered; and most of the pathogens associated with humans will have been destroyed. From here to the end of the room is an extraordinary panoply of life, ranging from microscopic bacteria, to higher plants, trees, fishes, and fresh-water molluscs. It's all of them working together, supported by human engineering. It is a living ecology, about to be woken up.

(John Todd, designer of The Living Machine, at the opening ceremony, 13 October 1996, cited in Conference proceedings, *Eco-Villages and Sustainable Communities* 1997: 63)

Newbold House

Newbold House is in the town of Forres. It comprises a large Victorian house with 7 acres of gardens. It has charitable status and is an educative centre and a small intentional community. Although it is financially separate from the Findhorn Foundation, it embraces the spiritual practice of that organisation and falls under its umbrella.

People

Staff members of these communities belong to **The Findhorn Foundation**, which is known internally as 'the family'. There are approximately 150 staff members. They receive a small allowance (around £75 per week). Not everyone that works for the Foundation is a member, and some receive higher remuneration. This was the cause of some discontent at the time of my visits in 1997 and 1998. Staff members work incredibly hard and are the backbone of the work departments. They have few personal possessions, usually from choice, and tend to see their work in terms of 'service' (see Chapter 5). In order to be a full member of the Findhorn Foundation, one needs to have negotiated an entry route that is fairly arduous (particularly in financial terms). There is some flexibility, but a typical route is thus: Experience Week, then Exploring Community Life and possibly Daily Practice or Life Purpose. These are all week-long courses. Next comes a 3-month experience of Living in Community. Then, following an interview, the Foundation Year Programme. The student pays for each of these stages, and as they work full time for the Foundation during this time, there is scant opportunity to earn income externally. One needs then to be able to pay for the courses and to sustain oneself. That said, food and lodging are part of the courses and so only a small amount of spending money is required. The next step (for some) is to apply for staff posts as and when they become available. Staff members are deeply committed individuals. Many choose after one or more of the steps to earn income externally and to become a part of the Open Community. Often this is due to financial constraints.

Open Community members offer some commitment (usually labour) to the Foundation on very flexible and varying bases. These people want to have a connection with the Findhorn Foundation, but not to fully commit all of their time and energies to it. Some of the people running business from the sites are Open Community members. Those who offer a minimum of three shifts a week in a work department can be included in community-wide decisions.

Guests are a major source of income for the Foundation and most stay at Cluny in the first instance. There are many ways to visit and I found my visits personally enriching. Examples include the fully structured courses mentioned above, or 'work-exchange schemes' (labour for food and or lodging), or simply as a paying guest in bed and breakfast at the Park or Findhorn Bay Caravan Site.

People's motivations for visiting and joining the Findhorn Foundation are, of course, varied. However, there were recurrent trends in people's accounts of why they had either not left Findhorn, or had returned to the place more than once. Each interviewee spoke of a pull, and sense of affinity for the place.

> I just had to come back. I missed it once I got home.
>
> > (anonymous guest, 21 July 1997)

> This is the place for me.
>
> > (Wendy, Living in Community Programme, 1 January 1998)

> The first time I arrived here, getting off the train in Forres and coming up here, I just had a kind of sense of coming home.
>
> > (Patrick, Staff member, Cluny Garden, 3 January 1998)

> I just visited for a day and thoroughly enjoyed it for some reason. ... so I came up and did an Experience Week and it was one of the most amazing experiences of my life.
>
> > (Tim, Open Community, 4 January 1998)

Many short-term guests return annually to 'recharge'. These are typically in high-stress, high-powered professional and commercial occupations. Those undertaking one or more of the steps outlined above (towards, perhaps, membership) cite 'the community', 'people', 'ecology' or/and 'the spirituality' as important factors in their decision. These overlap:

> I think it's about integration, about something that wasn't working for me before I came here, and it was a sense of how the many bits to my life –

which I thought important – didn't work together. My life was a series of bits, and there wasn't a harmonious relationship between them, you know, there was my work and there was my spiritual life and there was my relationships: my family life, my relationship with nature, my creativity, my sexuality they didn't seem to cross over for me. What I see here and what I'm exploring is how to synthesise and bring those together so that there's harmony within that, because for me that's what focus is to my life. How can I work and be creative and be connected with the divine?

(Simon, student on Year Programme, 3 January 1998)

The most important thing for me is the intent to bring spirituality into everyday practices, basic everyday living and also there's a willingness to deal with the emotional issues in my life and other people's lives and how that works in a team.

(Tim, Open Community, 4 January 1998)

Routine and business

Cluny and The Park

This is complicated, and an introduction to some of the Foundation's business networks is given in the section 'Connections with other bodies' below. The aim of this section is to provide a feel of the routines of daily life for those living at and visiting Cluny and The Park. First, life is varied and many different activities occur simultaneously. There are probably over a 1000 people staying, living and working at the Findhorn Foundation at any one time.

Staff members are generally attached to one of the work departments. These include the Guest Department (which runs programmes such as Experience Week, which first-time visitors are requested to attend), Cluny and The Park each have Kitchens, Gardens (there is also Cullerne Garden), Maintenance and Homecare departments. Other departments include Communications, and Accommodation. For more detailed accounts of the work, see Chapter 4.

Guests who are taking part in the short introductory programmes all work as part of their experience of the community. This is usually in one of the following: the Kitchens, Gardens or Homecare departments. Other time will be spent with the group. The only people who do not work are those on full-time workshops. People generally work attentively in a relaxed atmosphere.

Within the day are certain structural conventions. Meditation is one – another is Taize singing. These occur in all Foundation-related communities and establishments worldwide, at the same time – morning, noon and early evening. Breaks are scheduled into the working day to permit sufficient time to attend these. 'Attunements' are another convention. At the beginning of each work session (usually 9–12, 2–5) the group working together 'attune' to the task at hand. This involves clasping hands, usually in a circle, and a silent meditation or prayer for a few seconds. It is a focusing exercise, which occurs also before meals. Meals are an institution and are communal in one of the two kitchens. Attuning is part of the Findhorn Foundation's work ethic: expressed in the slogan 'work is love in action'. It aims to integrate the different aspects of human 'being' in line with a holistic worldview. Thus, 'spirit' and 'love' are integrated into work – hence the stress at Findhorn on 'service'. Attunements are led or guided by the 'focaliser' (manager) of the work department, or sub-department.

Newbold House

> Newbold is very much like the Foundation, but with its own special flavour. It has its own membership scheme and runs its own workshops.
>
> (Riddell 1996: 195)

Income is mainly generated at Newbold from the hosting of workshops and retreats. Examples are cultural workshops such as 'Sacred Dance' 'True Voice Singing' and counselling skills like 'Transforming Problems into Happiness' and psychosynthesis. It is relatively small and hosts just twenty-five resident guests at a time. Because of its size it affords a more intimate atmosphere.

Connections with other bodies

Minton House

Minton House is located near The Park. It is a not an intentional community. Nor is it located on Foundation territory or part of the Foundation's financial network. Rather, it is a bed and breakfast with a difference. It hosts up to twelve guests at a time:

> We place an emphasis on offering opportunities for worship and shared spiritual practice through weekly Taize singing, a meditational Eucharist, Yoga and Universal Peace Dances, and through our celebration of the Christian and Celtic festivals.
>
> (The Findhorn Foundation, Core Programmes, 1999: 19)

Minton House hosts retreats and offers respite care. It houses three projects: Music Thanatology (Music for the Dying), The Alanna Trust (which focuses on 'conscious living') and the College for Forgiveness. It is an independent entity, with connections to the Foundation:

> Judith Meynell, who owns Minton, sees it as supplementing the Foundation's work by providing a space where people can calm and rebalance themselves, with advice and support if necessary.
>
> (Riddell 1990: 199)

The Park

There is a cluster of small businesses sited at The Park. These include the café, mentioned above. Another is the Findhorn Bay Apothecary, which is a worker's co-operative. New Findhorn Directions is also centred here. This was established in 1979 and has been the administrative centre from which connected businesses are run. These include the Findhorn Bay Caravan Park, and The Phoenix Shop. These are businesses that have no charitable status. There are also independent businesses, which have no official connection to the Foundation, yet are based here. These have historically included a computer firm and a heating engineer (specialising in solar panels).

Two of these associated concerns are of direct relevance to the subject of this book. These are EarthShare and Trees for Life. EarthShare is the point at which I observed most direct contact between The Findhorn Foundation and the wider local community. By this I do not mean the thousand or so Open Community members, but the previously established community around Forres and Findhorn village. Generally, contact is quite limited and relations have historically not been intimate. Suspicion, wariness and resentment at the lack of financial interaction are apparent from some townspeople. There is, I believe, a renewed attempt to overcome some of this. EarthShare is one practical way in which this might be achieved. It consists of co-operative farming and land ownership of plots and fields in the area. Farming practices are organic and labour intensive. Participants in introductory courses at Cluny and The Park work on this land, as do people from the wider community. In the case of the former group, it is offered as part of their community experience: whole fields are weeded by hand as 'group projects'. The latter work as part of a labour exchange. EarthShare runs an organic vegetable scheme, which provides seasonal vegetables and fruit. Labour forms part of the currency of exchange in this scheme. It is described as an attempt at greater interaction with the wider community and at sustainable farming. Work is done in the same atmosphere and conditions as in the internal Foundation work departments. Attunement precedes the allocation and selection of tasks, and work is guided (led) by a focaliser.

Trees for Life is another small charitable organisation. It was established in 1987. It is based at The Park, but does its (physical) work some distance away in the centre of the highlands: mostly in and around Glen Affric. Trees for Life aims to regenerate the Caledonian Forest. This involves, in the first instance, several extensive replanting schemes. In the spring of 1997, for instance, 25,000 Scots pines were planted within a 187-hectare enclosure in Glen na Ciche, by Athnamulloch, 15,500 birch, rowan, eared willow and Scots pine at Carnach Mor, and aspen was established in several sites around Glen Affric and Glen Moriston. Riparian willow is being re-introduced along the Affric River. Largely volunteers do this work, and Sally and Paul Kendall, formerly long-time volunteers, administer the project. Funding comes from a number of sources. These include members and individual supporters, as well as Scottish Natural

Heritage and the Millennium Forest for Scotland Trust. Trees for Life work in close co-operation with what was the Forestry Commission, now Forest Enterprise.

In addition to this replanting, Trees for Life has a radical goal. Their aim is not simply the re-integration of trees into their indigenous habitat, but the development of an entire ecosystem. Species such as the pine marten, capercaillie and Scottish crossbill, grasses and plants and even larger mammals – beavers, moose and even lynx, wolves and bears are part of the long-term vision:

> The long-term ecological health of the Caledonian Forest requires the return of missing species such as the wolf. . . . Each species should be returned to the wild as and when suitable ecological conditions are established for it.
>
> (Trees for Life Newsletter, *Caledonia Wild!* Summer 1997)

This is a far-reaching project that is expected to require longer than the life of the trees to reach maturation (250 years). Work involves the spiritual practice and management style of other Findhorn Foundation activities. Practical ecology is informed by environmental ethics. These combine with New Age or deep ecological attitudes to life in their principles of ecological restoration:

1 Mimic nature wherever possible.
2 Work outwards from areas of strength, where the ecosystem is closest to its natural condition.
3 Pay particular attention to 'keystone' species.
4 Utilise pioneer species and natural succession to facilitate the restoration process.
5 Re-create ecological niches where they have been lost.
6 Re-establish ecological niches.
7 Control and/or remove introduced species.
8 Remove or mitigate the limiting factors which prevent restoration from taking place naturally.
9 Let nature do most of the work.
10 Love has a beneficial effect on all life.
> (Paul Kendall, Trees for Life website: http://ww.gaia.org/treesforlife)

Of this latter, they say:

> *Love has a beneficial effect on all Life*: This is perhaps the one unique principle which we work with at Trees for Life, and it stems from one of the early experiences of the original Findhorn garden in the 1960s. . . . This principle underlies all our work, as we know that love nurtures the life force and spirit of all beings, and is a significant factor in helping to heal the Earth.
>
> (*ibid.*)

This is an example of practical ecology (or permaculture) with a spiritual ethos. This combination characterises all of The Findhorn Foundation's ecological projects. Findhorn is an archetypal New Age community, crafting eclectic spiritual practice and ethos with transformative and charismatic politics. Some ground is shared between the New Age worldview and that of deep ecology. This is explored further in Chapter 5. The association of the New Age with green politics is not discouraged at Findhorn. One of Trees for Life's publicity leaflets, for instance, carries the following endorsement:

> Trees for Life is an excellent project. Healing wounds that we've inflicted on Planet Earth will not happen by magic, and regeneration projects of this kind have a crucial role to play in that process. It's both practical and visionary – and it needs your support!
>
> Jonathan Porritt

The Isle of Erraid

Physical space

Erraid is a small tidal island of one square mile, which lies by Mull off the West Coast of Scotland. It is stunningly beautiful. The community occupies a 5-acre plot, containing eight former lighthouse keepers' cottages. The lighthouses, built by the original occupants from granite quarried from Erraid, can be seen on the horizon. Behind each cottage is an outdoor compost loo. The island consists of a 'mini-highland' coastal biosphere: granite base with peat bog, silver sand and malchair such as is found on the coastal islands. There are blackfaced sheep and two dairy cattle. The community is a satellite of the Findhorn Foundation, with financial autonomy. It does not own the island, which is the property of a Dutch family unconnected to the Foundation. The relationship between the owners and the occupants is one of caretaking: the family has access to the island and take possession of it for 2 months each summer. Otherwise, only the community and their guests occupy the island. The community was established in 1978.

People

At the time of my first visit to Erraid, in the summer of 1997, the numbers were low, and the community consisted of six adult members and one child. Since then more have joined and the community is at its optimum size of ten. It is one of the smaller communities visited during research for this book.

Membership of the Erraid community consists of a similar, but flexible version of the requirements of the Findhorn Foundation. Some members come to Erraid after living at Cluny or The Park, seeking a more intimate context. All of the members of the Erraid community speak of the island and its ecology as part of their reason for joining the community:

> I visited Findhorn about five times before I came here and what put me off the community was that it was too small and I didn't like the people ... But I really love the island ... I always came for 1 week and whenever I left it just really felt like a wrench
> (Katie, member of Erraid community, 29 August 1997)

Katie lived at the Findhorn Foundation for 5 years before joining the community at Erraid. Elizabeth's experience was similar, although her motives differed:

> I have lived at Findhorn. I appreciate the teachings, but don't want to be involved with teaching people; also I wanted a smaller community, also animals. This is a very holistic community: balanced. ... Things that I like most are the view from the street. When it's working I like that sense of synergy – a sense of 'spiritual in touchedness' really.
> (Elizabeth, member of Erraid community, 27 August 1997)

Others are attracted to Erraid itself without prior knowledge of the Foundation. Peter, for instance, came initially as a guest, having never encountered Findhorn:

> As a guest I was attracted by the place and the nature. I had an inkling it'd be interesting to stay and I started coming back for longer in an open-ended way. Nature, being outside, the work ... it's been a gradual process.
> (Peter, member of Erraid community, 28 August 1997)

Peter's main attraction was to the ecological aspect of this community and not to the spiritual teachings of the Findhorn Foundation. People who come by this route are required to attend an Experience Week prior to commitment to membership. Members are asked to commit to stay for a minimum of a year. Each member 'focalises' activity on the island for a week at a time. This involves leading morning mediations and meetings. In addition, each member has specific responsibility for an area of work – examples are the vegetable garden and the candle workshop.

Routine and business

Erraid generates income from two sources: guests, and the sale of candles. It is, as far as is practicable, self-sufficient in terms of food production (some grains and dry stuffs are externally purchased). The gardens at the front of the cottages yield the vegetables that form the main staple of the diet. Food production is labour-intensive and low-tech and the working day is structured along the same lines as the Findhorn community, and is rigidly adhered to. Guests work alongside members.

Days begin with singing in the community's sanctuary at 8 a.m., which is followed at 8.30 by a led meditation. There is then a meeting in which sharing ('Today I feel ...') and attunement take places. Guests are offered various work opportunities and asked to 'attune to' (choose) one of these. Work commences after the meeting and breaks off for meditation at noon, and lunch. The afternoon shift is from 2 to 5 p.m. Meditation is very much a part of the working day here, as with the Findhorn Foundation community. Guests have free time on a Wednesday, whilst 'the family' have a meeting. There is a strong sense of separation: guest from member in this community, although guests stay in the homes of the members. It is at once intimate and distant. Fridays are cleanup days (for the next week's guests) and the evening is offered as space for 'play': dance, storytelling and singing.

The stress, in everyday life, is on a holistic balance of work and spiritual practice and on open communication with others. The community attempts to work sympathetically with their ecological environment. This includes planting appropriate crops and extends to an attention to 'spirit'. Some pay attention to lunar cycles in ordering their planting. Others speak of a connection with the spirit of the plants. It is a harsh environment in which to live this way.

Connections with other bodies

I have already mentioned the connection to Findhorn, and guests at the latter are encouraged to visit Erraid. Members of the Foundation can visit for a holiday. During my stay, for instance, the Foundation's Health and Safety Officer visited the island. Links are quite close although the island community asserts its autonomy. There is a small candle-making business in one of the workshops behind the cottages. Candles are made by hand and guests can assist in this. The candles are sold at Cluny and in the Phoenix Shop at the Park. These appear to be the only retail outlets.

Iona Retreat House

There is, on the Isle of Iona, by Mull, a retreat house that is affiliated to the Findhorn Foundation, and the Erraid community has close connections with this. Guests at Erraid are invited to visit the retreat on their free day (Wednesday).

Life on Erraid is an attempt to live the principles of holism and integration in a context that is close to nature. It shares these aims with deep ecology. The stress here is on putting into practice these ecological and spiritual principles. This, it is hoped, will ground sustainable living. Guests are welcomed here, as with Findhorn, not only as a source of income, but also because they form a central part of the community's educative and transformative mission. Literature produced by the Findhorn Foundation is replete with statements of world-changing intent:

> The Findhorn Community in northern Scotland is based on a strong faith that the world and people and living can indeed be different.
>
> (McVicar in Caddy 1994: 7)

This, it is thought, occurs initially with the inner transformation of the individual:

> Take that leap into the New without hesitation and simply know that it will be wonderful, far more wonderful, than what you have left behind in the old. With change comes life, a full and glorious life.
>
> (Caddy 1994: 42)

And Findhorn is seen as a critical mass of transformation:

> We are a beacon of light, shining across the world.
>
> (Publicity leaflet)

Beech Hill Community

Physical Space

Beech Hill Community live in a large house in rural Devon with various outbuildings (including the most salubrious compost loo) and 7 acres of organically maintained gardens. These include a vineyard, several formal gardens, a fruit garden and a paddock. The paddock is used by campers and contains a solar shower. When I visited in 1997, a reed-bed sewage system was being designed and installed by some of the members. The house and buildings are well maintained. The ownership of the property is mixed; some being owned co-operatively, some privately, and some in Trust. The community was established in 1983.

Members have their own living spaces, which range from a flat to a bedroom. The communal space is welcoming and attractive. Meals are taken communally in the evenings and at weekends. There is a communal lounge and several bathrooms. Guests stay in a newly refurbished wing. It is hoped that this space will prove an income-generating asset.

People

There are fifteen adult members of this community, and three children. Potential members are invited to visit on 'visitor weekends' in the first instance. This institution is common amongst intentional communities and allows the everyday life of the community to continue relatively undisturbed for most weeks of the month and concentrates visitors to a manageable space of time. If the initial visit is a success, then a return visit on the same basis is encouraged. Then a 2-week visit is followed by a probationary period of 6 months. Membership is not a guaranteed outcome of this process.

Membership entails, amongst other things, a commitment to work for the Co-op for a minimum of 5 hours a week. This might be in one of the sub-groups (gardening, maintenance and administration). Saturdays are 'workdays' when the community (and any visitors) work together on any ongoing projects. Most members also work externally to the community in professional occupations.

The community is self-described in the following terms:

> To live here happily and effectively, people need goodwill, personal initiative, tolerance and stability. . . . The co-operative's aims are summed up as follows:
>
> - to achieve maximum flexibility for individuals within collective policies;
> - to create structures and opportunities which maximise possibilities within the current social and economic climate;
> - to be aware of the impact of our work and lives on the environment and to develop projects accordingly.
>
> (Coates *et al.*, *Diggers and Dreamers* 1996/7: 173)

Routine and business

This community operates by an internal democracy. Decisions regarding the community are taken by consensus at weekly meetings. There is a voting system of simple majority, which operates under rare circumstances. Only full members have a vote. The Community is currently recovering from serious financial crisis and this accounts for the complex ownership patterns here. Beech Hill Property Holdings Ltd (a Trust) own the land freehold. This company also owns some of the units in the main house. Individuals either have leasehold or tenancy. A Co-operative runs the land: Beech Hill Community Co-op. Their aim is to eventually own all of the property.

This is not an income-sharing Co-operative. There is a 'food pool', to which each contributes a weekly sum of around £10. There is also a 'car pool' in which six people share two cars. Heating and maintenance costs are met by contributions.

Connections with other bodies

The community offers their paddock as host space for gatherings and conventions of ecological organisations. Friends of the Earth had, for instance, visited in the summer of 1997. An annual Open Day is held to which the wider community is welcomed, and this community has good relationships with their local community. They host and co-ordinate a Community

Composting Scheme, which is sponsored by the Local Authority. They belong to a Community Recycling Scheme. Contacts with the Local Exchange and Trade System (LETS) are active. They also participate in the Local Agenda 21 Scheme. These networks are subject to discussion in Chapter 3. For now, they serve to illustrate the informal but manifold contacts that this community has with other neighbourhood and national environmental organisations.

Blackcurrant Community

Physical space

Blackcurrant is an urban housing co-operative that owns two houses in Northampton, where it has been located since 1988. It is the only urban community included in this book. Despite its setting, it has some environmentalist links. Further, it was the founder member of an organisation called Radical Routes, which provides support and funding for intentional communities.

One of the houses is occupied by rent-paying tenants on a commercial basis. This is an income-generating concern. The other is home to the intentional community. The latter is a large townhouse with workshops and a garden. It was formerly a school. Communal space includes the old schoolroom, which is used also by a local-community theatre group, and a large open-plan kitchen and dining room on the ground floor. The workshops are also shared space and, at the time of my visit, were being used by one member for bodging and other traditional woodcrafts.

People

At the time of my first contact with Blackcurrant in 1997, the community had seven full adult members and three resident children. There has been some turnover of membership since then and the community is now slightly larger. The membership process is similar to that at Beech Hill: initial short visits, an extended trial period and then possibly membership. Community members decide this by consensus.

Most people work externally to the community on a part-time basis in order to generate income. For instance, Ian works for a local newspaper and Guff (who has subsequently left) worked at a home for young offenders. Dru is a student. Members take responsibility for specific areas of community life. Examples are maintenance, and accounts, and work internally is – in theory – equitably distributed. The community run an organic vegetable delivery scheme – of which more in Chapter 3.

The ideological focus of this community is self-described as 'co-operative'. Individual members describe themselves as holding anarchist, socialist and ecological worldviews.

Routine and business

There is no identifiable routine in this community, although they are extremely organised as a business. Ownership is co-operative and fully mutual. This is explained further in Chapter 4. Briefly though, members do not need to contribute money prior to joining the co-op (a token sum of £1 buys indemnity). Upon joining, each becomes an equal part of the ownership of the property. This status is relinquished upon leaving. All pay rent (to the co-operative) in order to meet mortgage payments. Membership includes voting rights and a commitment to maintain the community and its premises.

Food is purchased collectively and this is a vegetarian community.

Connections with other bodies

The community has good informal relationships with its local community. An example of this is their willingness to lend tools and machinery to local residents; Ian: 'Well, we're so well equipped. You can do that when there are a lot of you, it's so cheap. We're happy to let people share our stuff' (1 August 1997). The organic-vegetable scheme is a co-operative business, run by some members. This also involves interaction with the community, and involves the provision of high-quality, low-cost produce. In interviews this was explicitly linked to the desire to encourage organic and sustainable farming.

Radical Routes

This community is Secretary to Radical Routes and administers much of this organisation's publicity material. Radical Routes comprises a network of co-operatives. It raises loan stock to enable co-operatives to buy their property. Their ethos is co-operative and political. They work with sympathetic financial institutions, such as The Co-operative Bank, and with individuals who want to engage in 'ethical investment'. Their aim is social change. Their mission statement is as follows:

> We are creating bases from which to resist and challenge dominant structures in society and aim to develop an alternative economy and way of living. Through close co-operation we are taking control over property and land, developing economic and educational ventures and community based projects, all with the aim of empowering people at grassroots level.
>
> (Coates *et al.*, *Diggers and Dreamers* 1996/7: 209)

This explicit commitment to social transformation speaks to the discussion in the previous chapter of the functions of utopian thought. I identified transgression – breaking with convention – as having an important role in transformative utopianism. The deliberate challenge here to patterns of property ownership and 'dominant structures' is an act of transgression in this sense. It permits Radical Routes and the communities associated with it to begin to build new structures of exchange and ownership and, consequently, new ways of living in society.

Environmental politics is not central to this community's ethos. It is included in this book because of its historical importance in the co-operative movement. As such it is referred to for information regarding co-operative ownership. It is, however, not treated as a source of deep ecological consciousness.

Earthworm Community

Physical space

Earthworm Community is in Shropshire, at 'Wheatstone', which was formerly a large family house. It is now quite ramshackle and is recovering from a period of difficulty, which involved another community that formerly occupied the property. Earthworm was started in 1990. It has 7 acres of land. This includes three vegetable and herb gardens and open areas that are used for camping. There is also an area that is part of the International Peace Field (see Chapter 3).

The gardens are run according to principles of veganism. No animal matter or compost is used. There are outbuildings, which contain a flat and offices, as well as log stores and compost loos. This was the only community that had a separate outdoors 'wee-pit': a straw-filled space for urination.

Most community members live inside the house, but there are also caravans and a bus in the gardens.

Internally, the house is high ceilinged and spacious with two staircases. There is a small kitchen and a communal dining room. Other communal rooms include a television room, a smoking room, a meeting room, bathrooms and a ballroom (this was being used as an onion store at the time of my visit).

People

This is a friendly and relaxed community with more female than male members. Members are politicised and active, although several included auto-critique during interviews regarding their lack of organisation. Membership is by the same route as the two above mentioned communities.

Routine and business

This is housing co-operative. It raises its own loan stock. Another community formerly occupied the house, and several of these had been evicted, and the community was attempting regeneration at the time of my visit in 1998.

Each member has responsibility for a part of the house (e.g., the kitchen, the vegetable garden) and related tasks. Cooking is done in turn and meals are eaten communally.

Connections with other bodies

Politically, this community is ecologist and members have connections with the more radical fringes of green politics. Members have various histories of activism in Direct Action and the dance and rave scenes. Several come from a squatting or travelling background.

The community hosts gatherings (e.g., of the Animal Liberation Front), and rents its fields to campers. Connections to other environmental organisations tend to be informal. The community describes itself thus:

> We aim to explore and promote ecological and sustainable lifestyles. We try to minimise our use of products involving human, animal, and environmental exploitation.
>
> (Coates *et al.*, *Diggers and Dreamers* 1996/7: 154)

Like many of the communities referred to in this book, Earthworm acts as a host to WOOFERS: Willing Workers on Organic Farms. This is an organisation that aims to facilitate travel and to promote organic farming. Members visit participating farms (and intentional communities) and exchange labour for food and accommodation. The community hosts workweeks for big projects such as tree planting.

Relations with the local community are not historically good at Earthworm. This is partly due to the drug culture generated by previous occupants: 'It got stripped by smackheads about 6 years ago' (Gaia, Earthworm, 7 October 1998).

Talamh Community

Physical space

The house at Talamh is a medieval farmhouse, which retains 50 acres of land. This land is carefully managed as a species habitat, and contains also a young permaculture garden, a polytunnel and herb gardens. It is sited in Lanarkshire, near the M74 between two open-cast mines. It was established in 1992, and is the youngest of the communities included in this book.

There are barns and outbuildings. In one barn is 'the library' a space used for social meetings, music and dancing. Another contains the community's offices. There are compost loos and a sauna.

Practical ecology is an important activity at Talamh. The land is quickly reverting from rye grass (heavily grazed farmland) to a more sustainable and bio-diverse condition. There are two sections of woodland that the community are coppicing and re-planting. Old spruce is cleared and mixed broadleaved trees are being introduced. The woods now contain rowan, hazel, willow, oak and ash, in addition to conifers. There is a wetland area, with a naturally occurring marsh, at the end of which a pond has been made. The regeneration of the land is according to a simple principle: 'You just pick what's good, keep it good, and improve the rest' (Ian, 9 August 1997). Common soft rushes for instance were prolific in the wetland area. These have been retained, whilst space was cleared for valerian and meadowsweet. In another area a stream runs through a small hollow – this is reserved as a quiet place.

People

There were fifteen adult members of Talamh community when I visited in 1997. Five friends had founded the community 5 years previously. It was initially income pooling and privately owned. Talamh is a lively and welcoming community. It is ecological in outlook, combining practical ecology and land management with an unpretentious holistic lifestyle. Individuals follow their own spiritual practices, but the community is not defined in these terms. Members include practitioners in alternative health, including shiatsu and herbalism.

> A lot of time went into building the sauna. Really if we're here with the aim of promoting sustainability, that's actually looking after yourself, you know. Looking after yourself means feeding yourself, keeping yourself warm, but also means looking after yourself healthwise, and so we want to promote alternative health. And it also means being able to look after your recreation and you and your neighbours need to know how to enjoy yourself. And so our workshops would include drama workshops and drumming and dance, as well as passing on ideas on renewable energy and organic gardening.
>
> (Ian, 9 August 1997)

Routine and business

Talamh is co-operatively owned. The community raises loan stock. It was, at one time, income sharing. Now members pay rent to the co-op. It has had fully mutual co-operative status since joining Radical Routes in 1996. Income is generated by educational workshops. The community runs a voluntary conversation organisation.

Members each have responsibility for specific areas – such as the herb garden or the vegetable plot, or administration. A lot of energy and time is put into outreach work and the community's stated aim is to promote and sustain an eco-logical lifestyle.

Connections with other bodies

Talamh is a member of Radical Routes. It offers its space to community network events and hosts gatherings and political events. Every year there is a community volleyball tournament at which intentional communities gather, and they hosted this in 1996. The Direct Action group 'Earth First!' has used Talamh for an annual gathering.

This community makes efficient and effective use of volunteer workers. Much of the tree planting has been funded by woodland grant schemes and Talamh Community has planted the trees with the help of volunteers. This has been achieved through organised 'Volunteer Weeks'.

Talamh has good links with local schools, scout groups and colleges. It has established a small permaculture garden at the local primary school. Outreach and education in ecology and co-operation are primary aims of this community. It seeks to facilitate, encourage and enact an ecological lifestyle.

People in Common

People in Common (PIC) now live in a former corn mill on the banks of the Lancashire Calder. This co-op started life in Burnley in several separate houses but is now based at 'The Mill', which its members have converted to living accommodation, and the 5-acre garden. It is a well-established community, which began in 1973.

The Mill is huge and well cared for. The groundfloor contains workshops and a communal area that was formerly the boiler room. The first floor has a large kitchen and living space, which is shared. This is the vegetarian kitchen. There is also a television room and office on this floor. The second and third floors contain bedrooms, bathrooms and two more kitchens. Most members live in the Mill; two prefer caravans in the gardens.

This community contains some enthusiastic and expert gardeners. The gardens contain a polytunnel, vegetable and fruit plots, lawns, trees and flowerbeds. They are well maintained on organic principles. The River Calder runs around the perimeter of the gardens. There are always new projects for improvement underway. There are, for instance, plans to establish compost loos in the gardens.

A hardwood co-operative operates from the site. This utilises sustainably gathered (waste) hardwood. It is further discussed in Chapter 4.

People

At my first visit, PIC had eight adult members. It has since expanded. There is a wide age range in this community and a mix of experienced communards and first-timers. It is a friendly and vibrant community. Membership is by invitation following a trial period and, as with communities above, members have specific responsibilities for communal maintenance and upkeep, as well as voting rights.

Routine and business

This is a fully mutual housing co-operative.

Connections with other bodies

This is a well-established community within the communal network. It is not a member of Radical Routes.

This community has active and mostly informal connections with the local community. The children attend the local school. Most adult members work externally to the community. Some work for the workers' co-operative that is on site (this is discussed in the subsequent chapters). These connections have generated good external relations that range from the formally political: the Henry Doubleday Research Organisation – an international organisation that aims to 'promote, research and demonstrate organic horticulture and agriculture in the UK' (publicity leaflet), the Cuba Solidarity Campaign, local socialist groups – to community action charities and networks. Some members engage in voluntary youth work. The community also has informal connections with other environmental organisations, such as Greenpeace.

Conclusion: utopian bodies?

In these intentional communities, pragmatism combines with idealism. They share a desire for a sustainable lifestyle. This is variously interpreted, but includes attention to one's impact on the local environment, and efficient use of resources (and this includes a co-operative ethos of material goods). Sustainable human relations are also aspired to, and here co-operation, sharing and respect are keywords in the interview transcripts. The concept of interdependence co-exists with that of individuality in these people's accounts of their life choices.

Intentional communities combine also political dissatisfaction with the imaginative creation of alternatives. The disaffection can be summarised as issuing from two sources. The first might be described as contemporary culture. All interviewees cited materialism and excessive individualism as part of their critique of contemporary society. In other words, a mindset or worldview was perceived to be at the root of such things as poverty, environmental degradation and other specifically identified social problems. This worldview is characterised by distance, separation, selfishness and greed.

> The big thing, I think, is the scale.... People are caught up in what's fashion-able: mobile phones, etc. The increasing use of resources, pressure to get into the market. Not enough research into cause and effects.
>
> (Elizabeth, Erraid, 27 August 1997)

From my understanding of modern society, what's gone wrong is that we've somehow managed to be conditioned and to sort of believe it. It doesn't allow us to get over our fears, to get rid of our attachments.

(Janie, Talamh, 9 August 1998)

The word that springs to mind is greed. Doing things without thought for other people, that's what's wrong with society.

(Derek, PIC, 7 December 1997)

The second source of discontent is the political and economic infrastructure. Structural political problems, such as inadequate representation or ineffective institutions, were connected in these accounts to a deeper malaise:

It's all too big really. I think actually, you know, talk about politics in terms of government and the way decisions are made, I think it's far too remote from actually the common people.

(Richard, Beech Hill, 12 September 1997)

There is a loss of contact. For instance, in politics, to vote once every few years for me there was a sense of loss of influence and only a negative sense of protest. One reason I wanted to live in a community was that I wanted to move away from negative protest towards something positive, something that was building.

(Elizabeth, Erraid, 27 August 1997)

The political systems and social systems don't actually match how the world operates. ... In the 1700s you've got a worldview that solidified around Darwinism and the survival of the fittest for which capitalism is the political and social system. ... One grows out of the other – people believe this is how the world works and so your political and social systems eventually mirror that belief. ... What I think is emerging now is a completely different worldview based on quantum physics, chaos theory, the whole ecology movement – that essentially we're all interdependent. This is not a negative thing, it's positive. I think we're at a point in history; there's a new worldview emerging in science and religion and philosophy that our political and social systems will take ages to catch up with.

(Chris, PIC, 12 December 1997)

All of the communities that are described above have links – often informal – with other environmental organisations. This might be in the form of individual friendships with, say someone in Greenpeace, which result in the community hosting a private meeting, or annual gathering. It might be that members of the communities belong to other organisations and hold office in them. Rarely do communities have institutional affiliations. However, the levels of political activity are high – there is, literally, always

ing happening, about to happened or just happened. This might be a planting weekend: many of these communities are committed to re-estation and biodiversity projects. It may be a Direct Action or protest. may be an international day of meditation.

> But actually I am very excited by the number of alternatives linking up, and which seem to have influence. ... A lot of agencies and organisations are creating new initiatives and ways forward.
>
> (Elizabeth, Erraid, 27 August 1997)

The scope and variety of activity is further pursued in the next chapter. I mention it now by way of introduction of another utopian theme: radical creativity. Utopian thinking is imaginative and creative. I have suggested that one lasting political function of utopias is that they provoke and provide spaces in which opposition can occur and in which it is possible to think and act differently. I connected this in Chapter 1 to paradigm shifts, and this is a theme of the rest of the book. Utopias are transgressive spaces in which rules can be broken and alternative arrangements imagined and explored (conceptually and physically). Intentional communities appear to be ideal places in which this can occur.

In this, then, one function of these communities might be said to be to contribute to the paradigm shifts in consciousness that are written about in the bodies of thought referred to in this book. The accounts are ideological, in that they have theoretical depth. This may not be sophisticated, or fully articulated, but it is nonetheless present. The statements cited here are from people who have thought about politics and society and taken some action, as they thought best, to try to change things for themselves and perhaps for others. When asked whether intentional communities have a role in bringing about their desired changes, all responded in the affirmative. For some, they have a demonstrative role:

> I think that they [intentional communities] have a role as an example of different ways of living where decisions and material things can be more shared. Where things can be more balanced. Where people's needs can be met. Quietly.
>
> (Peter, Erraid, 28 August 1997)

> I think the ability of people to get together, to collaborate and to create their own environments and their own lifestyles, which have an integrity unto themselves is one of the, I think, one of the biggest ways that change can be brought about. ... For me, to encourage that culture is a very powerful thing to do, not only to encourage diversity, but I think it's a liberation of the human spirit, it gives us the ability to be creative.
>
> (Simon, Findhorn, 3 January 1998)

Many were very modest about this, and saw their influence in local terms only.

For others, communities permit exploration:

> I think the more diversity there is, the more chance, the quicker we'll find what works in the way of people living together. What are the different tools that can help people to really live together harmoniously and have a meaningful existence? That's not, maybe, so heavily dependent on material possessions and begin, everyone separate. And I guess I think that it's also important that there is plenty of sharing of experience between different communities . . . hopefully people can find ways of solving their problems and try new approaches and get a sense of unity, a sense of support.
>
> (Patrick, Findhorn, 3 January 1998)

In these accounts the function is to display or show the possibility of a feasible alternative to private property, the nuclear family, full time work for wages, individualism, selfishness and other things cited in their critique. As such, they might be said to contribute to a (critical?) mass of opposition. This is a sub-theme of the discussions in the chapters that follow and is one reason why I have insisted on the value of including the range of sources in my research. Is there a body of opposition to the *status quo* that can provide the impetus and grounding for sustainable political change?

Finally, intentional communities are homes. They are places in which people have chosen to live and work together. They are more or less warm and welcoming. They contain the strife and struggles and mundanity of everyday life. They are where people – diggers, dreamers, malcontents and aspirers to a new and better way of life – actually live.

3   Publicising the private?

> Relationships here are in your face all of the time. There's no getting away from them.
>
> (Wendy, Findhorn, 1 January 1998)

Introduction

The separation of life into two conceptual spheres has become habitual and commonplace. We can, it seems, usefully think of our lives as occupying different spaces at different times: there is a public arena in which it is appropriate to do some things, and a private arena for others. Behaviour that is proper to one sphere may appear improper in the other. The nature and character of this behaviour often shifts to suit a given time and context.

Within liberal political thought, there is an identifiable tradition regarding these spheres. It is assumed that only one sphere: the public – is of political significance. The private sphere is valorised in early liberal accounts, and is protected from the interference of the state. In accounts such as John Locke's, for instance, 'politics' is an unattractive necessity of life. Life at home occurs in a sanctified space. Political and legal institutions function to protect private property and have no wider legitimate function. Interpersonal and sexual relationships, in this account, are private and non-political. Conservative thought also separates the private and the public, although slightly differently. For Edmund Burke, for instance, society is an organism: it contains elements that each have an essential role to play. This is natural and should not be interfered with (by politics or social engineering). Certain activities belong in the sphere of the state: law and order are examples, but only if they serve the interests of stability. It follows that a large range of activities (e.g., representatives' personal lives) is not politically significant. Indeed, it serves the interest of stability that most private institutions be left entirely unmolested.

This has a contingent effect on political culture. Within the British political tradition, for instance, the private morality of MPs or the Head of State may at one time be treated as literally unremarkable: private. In recent trends, the salacious nature of personal 'private' behaviour of 'public' figures is treated as politically significant. Can we trust an MP who lies to his wife? *Et cetera ad nauseam.* The private is thus publicised and made political. This issues questions of access to and ownership of the private lives of others. The 'right' of an individual to privacy often appears to be in conflict with the 'right' of 'the public' to knowledge.

Appropriate content, then, of the public and private spheres is historically and culturally specific – and formerly private matters are increasingly, it seems, becoming public property. Despite this, the conceptual separation of these spheres continues. Witness, for instance, the use of the terms in this discussion: private individual is opposed here to public collective: privacy is assumed to be the property of the individual, a 'right' against others, which requires legal protection.

A further consequence of the separation of public from private has historically been the exclusion of women and children from the political agenda. Feminist input into this debate is invaluable. Much feminist critique of Western political thought focuses on analysis of the public and the private spheres. Women, they say, have, in the modern period, been materially excluded from the public sphere in the concrete world of 'real' life. Sociological and empirical accounts of women's place in the workforce and in political institutions are a part of this analysis. So too is theoretical work, which suggests that the conceptual separation of public from private – and the association of women with the latter and men with the former – have legitimised this material exclusion. Carole Pateman expresses this concisely:

> Notwithstanding all the differences between theorists from Plato to Habermas, the tradition of Western political thought rests on a conception of 'the political' that is constructed through the exclusion of women and all that is represented by femininity and women's bodies. Sexual difference and sexuality are usually treated as marginal to or outside of the subject matter of political theory, but the different attributes, capacities and characteristics ascribed to men and women by political theorists are central to the way in which each has defined 'the political'. Manhood and politics go hand in hand.
>
> (Pateman 1988: 3)

It is my intention in this chapter to make the following suggestion: that consideration of intentional communities can problematise the ways in which we have become accustomed to thinking about the public and the private. The implications of this suggestion are manifold. It is indicative of the kind of thinking proposed in Chapter 1, in which several perspectives are focused on a single theoretical issue. Specifically, the practicalities of green (environmentalist) politics of lifestyle are brought into conversation with feminist theoretical analysis and deep ecological commitment to the holistic approach to problems.

This gestures a 'new' approach to thinking about politics that is transgressive and utopian. Intentional communities can help us to flesh out the imagined transformations of public and private that occur in feminist bodies of thought.

An approach to the public and private spheres which is both transgressive and utopian has implications for:

- the study of politics: the ways in which we might usefully and legitimately think about such concepts as citizenship, political agency and politics itself;
- the 'doing' of politics: the ways in which we behave, act, perform and live;
- the 'being' of politics: political identity – the roles and performances that we assume in the public–private (non-) political arenas.

Simply put, it enables us to think about ways in which the terrain of 'the political' changes and shifts.

The political, the public and the private

What is (not) political? Answers to this question shape the political agenda. Inclusion and exclusion of issues in the political sphere is, I suggest, a primary political act: it is (ontologically and chronologically) prior to political debate. It is constitutive of political discourse. The *polis* and the *oikos* correspond somehow to this. Often we unproblematically assume/accept that what is (not) political is what is private; that what is political is what is public. There is an irony at play here: the word 'ecologism' has its etymological grounding in the Greek word *oikos* (household). It is, then, a particularly appropriate place from whence to undertake this discussion.

Etymologically, of course, the 'political' is derived from the word 'politics'. Identifying the political should, then, be simple. Suppose, for the sake of argument, we assume a mainstream, traditional approach to the question and state that politics is about structures, systems and institutions: spaces in which publicly binding decisions are made. This is the definition assumed by many commentators on utopias. Krishan Kumar and J. C. Davies, for instance, both make this connection. For them, 'politics' (and thus utopias) are concerned with institutional–bureaucratic decisions (Kumar 1991; Davies 1984). It then follows that 'the political' is behaviour and activity that is appropriate to this space. Examples might be affairs of the state, distributive policy, geographical devolution of power and so on. Political actors in this account might be government executives or members of interest groups. Alongside this, suppose, in the name of argument, that we assume a radical feminist approach to the question. Now we can state that politics is about structures, systems and institutions: spaces in which privately binding decisions are made. The difference then in what might be considered 'political' is profound. Political actors might be husbands, fathers, wives and mothers; political issues might include sexuality, domesticity and the family. My interest here is in whether these two apparently opposing views are reconcilable.

(de)Construction of the public/private dichotomy

Deconstructive theory offers a useful account of the way in which politics is conceptualised. This suggests that the problem is in the approach to the process of conceptualising. This process is said to be driven by a logic of negation in which a concept is constructed by reference to what it is not. This process is the property of a dualistic and oppositional system of thought. Theories of dualistic thought haunt contemporary political thought. They influence the analyses of traditions as wide and varied as structuralism, post-structuralism, psychoanalytic theory, feminism and ecologism (plus, of course, any number of combinations of the above).

The 'basic' premise for most of these types of analyses is that there is a political relationship between language, thought and reality. The ways in which we express our reality – the ways in which we articulate ourselves and our experiences, are in other words, of political concern and contain or represent certain relations of power and domination. Between signification (representing a thing) and signified (thing) are thought to be a series or set of codes and laws and rules. The dynamic – or politically relevant character – of these systems of meaning and encodification varies within and between traditions. There is, in some accounts, assumed to be a reflective and reciprocal (but inequitable) relation between the process of constructing identity (gender, class, ethnicity, 'individual') and that of signification (Derrida 1977, 1978; Plumwood 1993; Cixous and Clement 1986). This is expressed with characteristic crypticness by Jacques Derrida as 'there is nothing outside the text' – *il n'y a pas de hors-texte* (Derrida 1977: 152–60). This approach assumes both that meaning is constructed by language and that language confers meaning on its subject. 'Meaning' in this account is connected intimately to cultural, social and political significance.

Two key assertions in these accounts concern binary linguistic oppositions. These are said to:

* Contain and often conceal relations of (dis)ingenuous hierarchy. 'Ecofeminist' Val Plumwood expresses this neatly:

   A dualism ... results from a certain kind of dependency on a subordinated other. This relationship of denied dependency determines a certain kind of logical structure, in which the denial and the relation of domination/subordination shape the identity of both the relata.

   (Plumwood 1993: 41)

* Be usefully approached through a process of deconstructive reading. Deconstruction *à la Derrida* involves a double and simultaneous move of inversion and subversion.

The discussion below adopts this approach in its reading of the public and the private with the aim of permitting something more interesting and politically useful to emerge. This is a deconstructive reading aimed at a transgressive and utopian end. I shall do this by initially privileging the private (inversion) and, as the chapter proceeds, by attempting to subvert the notion of separation of a political public from a non-political private.

Public and private

It is not my intention here to rehearse all the well-established critiques of public and private, which now constitute what might be called the relatively uncontested mainstream of feminist analysis. I shall, however, highlight a few points from this terrain that are salient to this current discussion.

Separation

The division of public and private spheres has been found to dominate liberal political thought (Shanley and Pateman 1991; Pateman 1988; Elshtain 1981). Briefly, as stated above, liberal political thought has theoretically separated the public from the private and asserted that politics is located in the former. This simultaneously devalues (politically) and values (as a sphere of precious sanctity) the private. Politics is important, and politics is dirty business. Women have, historically, been located in the private, whilst men travel between the worlds of work, money and power (public) and domesticity, love and relationship (private). Women thus sit excluded on their private pedestals in the accounts of canonical classical liberal thinkers and this, it is argued, has not been effectively acknowledged or negotiated within the liberal tradition.

Association

The material exclusion of women from the public realm has been accompanied by exclusion on the more covert level of conceptualisation. Women are associated with 'Woman' – a universalist construction whose defining characteristics are tendencies towards emotion, excess, concerns with the body, nature, etc. The point here is that these characteristics correspond to those considered appropriate to private behaviour and relations. Woman is thus written out of the public sphere. The legitimising strategies for this are manifold: naturalism, essentialism, biologism – all of which render woman conceptually invisible in the political public realm (Grosz 1990).

Implications

The particular distinction between the public and the private that developed with industrial capitalism in western societies resulted in women's exclusion from the 'rights' of citizenship and therefore constructed them as less than full individuals. The prevailing ideology was that men would govern the society and women the homes within it. The result was a model of social life that separated the 'private' domestic sphere from the 'public' sphere, reflected in and influenced by nineteenth century theory and the developing disciplines of the social sciences.

(McDowell and Pringle 1992: 15)

We can map the conceptual associations to which this passage refers thus:

public	private
active	passive
intelligence	intuition
rationality	emotion
politics	domesticity
wages	labour
Man	Woman

The gendering of the spheres of public and private activity corresponds to the political empowerment of the public and the impotence of the private. This positioning of concepts in binary opposition to one another has inevitable effects of closure and exclusion. From a feminist point of view, the implications of this run deep:

What is *male* becomes the basis of the Abstract, the Essential and the Universal, while what is *female* becomes accidental, different, Other.

Ecologists show how the separation of animals from humans has similar effects, being grounded in a logic of false negation. The sphere of the natural becomes intimately linked with that of the private and the Other (that which ought to be controlled). The assumptions and ontology of the social sciences, it is argued, further inscribe this into our (political) culture. A legitimising discourse of exclusion has thus been established.

Otherness

Intentional communities are a good place whence to review this relation and tradition, not least because they operate from a subjective position of otherness. I commented in Chapter 1 on the value of otherness to a utopian project of imagining. Utopia, the no place that is a good place, is an other-place. In terms of the broader society and culture in which they exist, intentional communities are strange, and different. They are the 'hippies on the hill', 'those weirdos'. Some people who live in intentional communities look 'different', unconventional: dreadlocks falling down their backs, they are wild and androgynous. In some cases, tattoos inscribe their bodies, and rings and studs pierce lips, brows, cheeks and noses. Often they strike a chord of exotic cultural dissonance in the rural settings of their community. Often they are judged accordingly: 'druggies', 'orgies', 'scroungers' and 'long-haired layabouts'.

This raises an interesting point regarding the privatisation of behaviour as 'non-political' and therefore not subject to political analysis. Anne Phillips has identified a number of interpretations of the slogan 'the personal is political', one of which speaks directly to this:

> Things that used to be dismissed as trivial can no longer be viewed as the haphazard consequence of individual choice, for they are structured by relations of power. Things once shrouded in the secrecy of private existence are and should be of public concern.
>
> (Phillips and Barrett 1992: 92)

Calling something non-political (private) renders it irrelevant to political discourse. Further, it disempowers the subject and denies her/him recourse. Commonly cited examples of this are drawn from the spheres of health and rehabilitation: madness and deviance. If behaviour can be constructed as deviant, then it can be medicalised and 'treated'. In this way it is privatised: rendered politically irrelevant and impotent. Suppose, for instance, we consider the actions of community dwellers to be merely deviant, their self-presentation to be merely wilful and/or self-destructive ('some of the girls are quite pretty, under all that muck, I don't know why they spoil themselves so'). Suppose we take this to be indicative of sloth, or as collectively dysfunctional. We might then construct them as victims of some maladjustment, as mad, as deviant, as requiring care, re-education: control. This is a danger of inhabiting a space of radical otherness.

Self-consciously situated outside of the mainstream then, as individuals and as collectives, community dwellers inhabit a position of alienated otherness. Also though, with this 'down side' (if indeed it is a down side) comes also the freedom within the space of the community to transgress, explore, rethink and rebuild ways of living and being and acting. All this coexists with the daily drudge of – whose turn to cook? Whose relationship just fell apart? Have we submitted the annual accounts?

My interest, in the remainder of this chapter, is to explore how people who have taken a conscious decision to live differently, according to their own 'politics', rules, codes and consciences, might live out alternative public/private relations. The home, in liberal thought, is the warm safe secure space of hearthside and family. The hounds of the state may be at the door, but the Leviathan is held in abeyance. What happens then when a home is a consciously and intentionally politicised space?

Internal public/private relations

Lifestyle as politics

Within (i.e., internal to) intentional communities, public/private relations are lived out in a number of interesting ways. Often issues relating to lifestyle connect to political and politicised activity. It is here that the politics of the ecological *oikos* become apparent. Examples are decisions about where and how to live and, within that space, how to deal with such 'mundane' and domestic matters as what to eat and how to dispose of domestic waste. My focus on the intimately domestic is deliberate. My aim is to develop a space in which these matters of ultimate privacy can be considered to be of relevance to the study of politics. My hope is that interesting things might then begin to happen to our conceptualisation of the politics.

Living in community is something that the adults with whom I spoke had consciously chosen to do. For some this was an explicitly ethical choice in which living has become part of an ethically informed process.

> For a long time I'd been interested in the concept of an intentional community, originally it was for sort of political reasons, and I had fairly strong left-wing politics when I was a lot younger, but the [Findhorn] Foundation is the only one that I've ever decided to go and visit – I've turned much more towards a spiritual understanding and, of course, that's what it's really known for ... the people, the place, the country, what's on offer, the social aspect, political aspect and a spiritual aspect, and – you know – it's pretty much all here for me really. So that's what drew me here.
>
> (Tim, Findhorn, 4 January 1999)

It is interesting to note in Tim's account a desire to integrate all significant aspects of his life. This is characteristic both of New Age thought and of deep ecology. Findhorn, for Tim, is a space in which this ideal can be explored.

For Janie, moving to Talamh was part of a similar desire for an integrated (or holistic) life in which work and home complement each other. The intimate nature of community living provides a context that she finds appropriate to open communication. This, she finds essential to her area of specialised work with youth in the wider community. Asked what attracted her to the community, she responded thus:

> I think it was that fact that I worked in youth schemes before. I worked in social work departments for years and I was just getting so frustrated with this feeling that I couldn't communicate with people because there were so many restrictions on what I could say and how you dealt with people and everyone became sort of figures ... I couldn't speak to them on a human level, because I had these sort of restrictions on what was acceptable and not acceptable in ways to work. .... Friends were telling me about this place and it just seemed like the ideal opportunity to work with people in that kind of way and to learn from people. Being open. And there wasn't some kind of boss or something to restrict the flow of communication between people. That's why I came here.
>
> (Janie, Talamh, 9 August 1997)

The community at Talamh is concerned to have an educative and demonstrative function. This was mentioned in Chapter 2. Outreach work is done with and in the local community – for instance, schools are invited to learn about biodiversity in their 50 acres of carefully managed land. This fact, alongside the nature of face-to-face relations, is what informed Janie's choice.

For others, the choice was made for reasons that are described in terms of personal considerations. Examples are broken marriages or relationships that necessitated a change in living situation. For yet others, the decision was informed by a housing crisis. The housing co-op, People in Common (PIC), was founded in Lancashire as part of the squatters movement in the 1970s. From London the organisation Shelter was seeking property in which to house homeless people – Chris and Derek, both of whom were still in residence at PIC in December 1997, came from this background, seeking radical solutions to an apparently insurmountable problem.

> Well, we started off as mostly people who'd been involved in squatting and were looking for a way of housing ourselves in better ways. I came to it with a worker's co-operative hat on and an industrial co-operative hat on as well. We originally agreed to look for a way to live together near a town, and at the time we were very concerned about sustainable agriculture.
>
> (Derek, PIC, 11 December 1997)

> It's difficult to know where to start, having been here for 19 years ... at different times it's been different communities, although I think there's been a thread running through it ... I joined here because I was a squatter – I came here through the squatting movement.
>
> (Chris, PIC, 12 December 1997)

A commonly cited desire is to live within something that feels like a family, or the desire to live in a big house with beautiful grounds which, under other circumstances, would be beyond their financial reach. This is often acknowledged:

> I think there's an aspect of communities that is nothing to do with political change. ... For a lot of people, it's – to put it cynically – it's 'nice place to live' syndrome. ... They can be a refuge for people who find it very hard in the outside world.
>
> (Chris, PIC, 12 December 1997)

However, living in community is not easy, and often those who apply to join hoping only for a good and easy life do not become full members. A certain commitment is necessary. Some people gave their initial reason for joining as contingency or non-political motives ('I split up with my partner' – 'I wanted my child to live somewhere rural') but/and then went on to speak with passion about their political beliefs and actions and ways in which community life enable these.

I was pregnant and needed to get out of London, 'cause I'd made a really conscious decision not to bring up a baby in the city ... I wanted to live and learn about the land ... people do come to the conclusion every now and then that you just can't live the way you've been living anymore, you've got to make a change, you've got to make a statement, you've got to do it.

(Gaia, Earthworm, 6 September 1998)

I think the main reason I wanted to join is that I have seen communities and visited a few and always liked the idea of living with a lot of people who are willing to live, eat and talk together and mostly help each other. I have always liked the principles of Communism but think things will stop true communism expanding over the world, but if I can live my principles it makes me feel a fuller person.

(Shaun, PIC, 17 November 1997)

Living consciously in this way, which involves taking stock and upping sticks and moving into (or forming) another community, is an act of political significance. Often the unusual nature of the public and the private was of direct relevance to a person's decision to live, in a given community. Most interviewees mentioned the intensity and openness of interpersonal relations as something to be confronted, challenged and, ultimately to cherish:

The most important thing is about having real meaningful contact with other people who aren't your partner and that sort of thing. I go out to work and chat with people but none of it actually gets very meaningful. Being in a relationship is very nice, but it's nice to have something else, something that falls between those two things.

(Ian, Blackcurrant, 2 September 1997)

In addition to the original motive of living communally, the process of living is, for many community dwellers, a political activity. When asked what, if anything, was wrong with modern society, several people gave answers that initially surprised me. These seemed 'trivial' matters. Examples are Sue, from Earthworm, who wanted to revolutionise toilets, and Katie, on Erraid, who also cited sewage disposal as a primary concern:

Well, I think it all stems from alienation, and if you're separated from your own body, what goes in your body, and what comes out of your body, and what your body uses in order to stay alive ... then you're profoundly alienated.

(Katie, Erraid, 26 August 1997)

Shit has been really important in my life. Composting shit has always been an important thing to me because I can't handle throwing it in the sea.

(Sue, Earthworm, 6 September 1998)

These statements were responses to questions concerning people's worldviews, desired changes and suggestions for achieving these ends. The compost loos at the Centre for Alternative Technology (CAT), Talamh, Earthworm, Beech Hill and Erraid are, I realised, not simply eco-fads, or issues of domestic convenience. Neither is the state-of-the-art reed-bed system that is being developed by Bunk at Beech Hill. They are all enactments of a worldview that stresses the connection of action and reaction, activity and product. A holistic consciousness of human impact on the planet is encouraged by the use of composting outdoor loos and wee pits. Of course, these things also have practical effects (e.g., the production of garden compost).

> Domestic sewage is potentially both a hazardous pollution-causing waste material and a valuable resource. .... All sewage has a vital role to play in the biological cycle of life, by the fertilising of the soil, upon which all life ultimately depends, life is sustained ... for instance, it produces compost and methane gas.
> (Centre for Alternative Technology, Composting sewage instruction leaflet)

What to eat is similarly, for some, of political and ethical import. Again, this forms part of an ecological holistic consciousness. Earthworm, for instance, is a vegan community. This reaches beyond food intake, as a note on the bathroom door reminds 'Veganism affects all aspects of life'. It involves discipline and consciousness in areas not often considered. Only 'ethical' products are used at this community:

> It's also about the use of ethical ingredients, cosmetics – nothing is animal tested. And also we do veganic gardening – we don't use any animal products in the garden.
> (Gaia, Earthworm, 6 September 1997)

Vegetarianism is linked in these accounts to a desired lifestyle that is in accordance with a worldview. It has ideological significance. This is in some cases deep ecological and in others environmentalist. The organisation Radical Routes was mentioned in Chapter 2. This is a support network that raises capital for communities who wish to buy their premises. Decisions at Radical Routes annual meetings are conventionally made by consensus. This includes decisions regarding the content of the code of ethics to which signatories subscribe. This specifies income levels of individual members (profiteering is not permitted) and other radical measures aimed at facilitating an alternative economy. In 1997, for the first time in years, a vote was forced. This was on the issue of vegetarianism: should the constituency be vegetarian and/or vegan communities? I mention this by way of noting the relative importance of such 'private' matters to the culture of intentional communities.

Recycling is another practical activity related to the domestic (private?) sphere that impacts on consciousness. Separating the organic waste from the inorganic, and the compostable from the non-compostable, is a deliberate activity that makes the agent of waste pause briefly for thought about what is being generated and how it is being disposed of, or used. At Beech Hill in Devon, recycling represents a connection to the wider community in the form of a community recycling scheme. Similarly, community compost schemes, such as that housed also at Beech Hill, serve to link the intentional community to the wider one. The link is in pragmatic environmentalist concerns and activity – but that which is shared exceeds this. These actions are politicised partly by their context: the fact that they occur in a consciously created and alternative space; partly by the impact they have on the wider community; and also by the consciousness of the actions themselves.

Further, they speak to ecological attempts to shift the paradigms of such concepts as efficiency. Fritz Schumacher was the first to fully articulate this view. He identifies an illusion which, he says, is at the centre of Western patterns of production and consumption:

> One of the most fateful errors of our age is the belief that 'the problem of production' has been solved. ... For the rich countries, they say the most important task is 'education for leisure' and, for the poor countries, the 'transfer to technology'. The arising of this error ... is closely connected to man's attitude to nature.
>
> (Schumacher 1974: 10)

He demands a shift in our patterns of consumption that is grounded in a different approach to nature. The practical methods of efficiency employed in intentional communities are illustrative of what this might look like in practice. This includes the re-use of clothes, waste (sewage and other domestic rubbish), as well as pooling large and energy-inefficient items:

> The more people you get, the cheaper it will be, so while this could be *more* efficient as a building, it's very efficient. As a method of transport we have a car pool and bikes, so that's very efficient. ... It's very well set up to be user friendly – a lot more than a normal house would be, and that's good.
>
> (David, PIC, 9 December 1997)

Lifestyle and issues of mundane day-to-day living are, within the context of the culture of community living, moments of politicised activity. Thinking about these issues in this way helps us to retain a sense of public and private whilst shifting the place of the political in and about and between both spheres. Awareness of this facilitates flexibility in the paradigms of the political. In this sense, then, thinking about life inside intentional communities provokes transgressive and utopian changes in the way that 'the political' is conceived.

Emotions

Certain forms of relationship have, historically, been considered inappropriate to the public sphere. These might involve such things as our 'personal' relationships: friendship, love and sexual relations. The feminist slogan 'the personal is political' has challenged this ghettoisation and indeed political philosophers have, since Aristotle, written about friendship (albeit between men). I propose here to focus on this in such a way as to draw upon feminist critiques of the depoliticisation of friendship, love and sex. These relations involve emotions and intimacy. Are emotions and intimacy appropriate only to the private? Alison Jagger says not. Her analysis begins in classically feminist terms:

> Typically, although not invariably, the rational has been contrasted with the emotional and this contrasted pair has been linked with other dichotomies. Not only has reason been contrasted with emotion, but it has also been associated with the mental, the universal, the public and the male, whereas emotion has been associated with the irrational, the physical, the natural, the particular, the private, and of course, the female.
>
> (Jagger 1989: 129)

She argues that emotions are, potentially, useful to a project of emancipatory politics because they are, or can be, epistemologically subversive. From a feminist standpoint it is clear that this might be an attractive political–epistemological strategy: re-valuing emotions (connected, as she argues, with Woman) is an act of subversive inversion of a dualistic binary.

How might this be pertinent to the politics of communal living? Emotions are close to the surface in many communities, and the sheer physical proximity of other people's day-to-day lives is apparent. In many of my interviews, prolonged accounts of personal relationships formed part of descriptions of the community. In several cases, emotions and personal relations were intertwined with the community's history – often the question: 'Could you describe this community for me?' resulted in something along the lines of: 'Well, Fred and Sue split and Sue left and then I got together with Fred and I moved in ...'. Emotions, and the ways that individuals negotiate relations in transition, are part of a community's history. They are part also of its character. The 'publicisation' of this is interesting. First, as stated, in community these negotiations are enacted in a fairly public space and frequently involve more actors than in a 'private' household. Indeed, several people cited the support of the community to be one of the most important things about being there. Second, the inscription of this into a 'code' of behaviour is often intentional and public. What constitutes 'appropriate' behaviour might be discussed, for instance, at a community meeting. This play of emotion on an (albeit contained) public stage is an integral part of what it is to live in community.

At the Findhorn Foundation an explicit connection has emerged between emotions, or inner private feelings, and the construction of an eth being. The development of an autonomous moral code is an impo₁ life in this community. The intentional community at Findhorn is player in the New Age Movement. It has an ecological and spiritua vision:

> The Findhorn Foundation honours divinity within all life through active service to God, humanity and nature to achieve individual and planetary transformation.
>
> (Walker in Seel 1997a: 8 and 21)

At Findhorn the 'inner self' is thought to be the authentic source of knowledge. Crudely put, the path to one's god is through listening for and to the voice of this inner self. Connections between 'religion', spirituality and politics are complex here as, within the emerging tradition of the New Age, the boundaries between these spheres are increasingly blurred. Spiritual enlightenment, guidance, and awakening are seen as routes towards personal and planetary transformation. The latter is thought to be impossible without the former. In this we can see an explicit expression of what I call transgressive utopianism. Boundaries are deliberately transgressed and a new space is created amongst things previously kept separate. In this space (this new place which was no place) radically new and creative thought and activity can, perhaps, occur. The function of transgressive utopian thinking is to both provoke and permit paradigm shifts in consciousness: thus enabling real sustainable change to be conceivable.

Ben Seel describes the Findhorn approach to this as 'individualistic expressivism' (Seel 1997a):

> Expressivism calls upon individuals to be 'true to themselves'; this means finding themselves and expressing themselves in a way that is somehow more authentic, natural, or better than the existing socially conditioned self. Expressivism, therefore, claims to be about liberating the individual from the bonds of socialisation.
>
> (Seel 1997a: 10)

The term often used to describe this is to 'follow your heart'. This clearly speaks to the disruption of the public and the private. We have here an approach which views the private inner self as a product in part of the external public, world. Further, we have an inversion, which re-values the private over and above the tainted public. Shades of Rousseau. Members of the Foundation speak variously of 'politics', and a recurrent theme of my interviews regarding this was an assertion that politics, as currently understood and practised, is neither sufficient nor appropriate to sustainably addressing the world's problems. This moves us beyond conceptual inversion: to a point at which new (anti-political?) transformations are being sought and practised. Something deeper, or prior, or more radical is required for lasting change. This applies across the board and was variously articulated by at least one interviewee in each community visited.

Where is the politics in this? Feminists have long suggested that emotions can be politically transgressive forces. Luce Irigaray and feminists of *ecriture feminine* posit sexual desire as a force of disruption in a system of linguistic codification. Less radical, but perhaps more applicable, here is Alison Jagger's suggestion above: that emotion *per se* has a role in the political sphere. Emotions can, she suggests, disrupt political paradigms. Inclusion of 'the emotional' alongside 'the rational' gives a fuller and more complex version of reality. People's emotional needs and connections with one another can be indications of the broader culture in which they are located. Terry, at Findhorn, expressed this in the simple desire:

> To have a society which accepts that men can show their feelings . . . and not just on the football field.
>
> (Terry, Findhorn, 2 January 1997)

Living in community often means giving space and respect to people that you do not terribly much like. 'Living in community is living closely with people that you might not choose as friends' – this is a wry joke amongst communards. In contrast, but simultaneously, communities are often described as intentional 'families'. At the Findhorn Foundation the term is explicitly used to refer to members. As noted above, the need or desire for 'connection' with others was often explicitly cited as a motivating factor when choosing a community. As with (many) families there is emotional support, emotional play and emotional conflict within communities. The differences though include two important factors: first, membership is in constant flux; second, membership is voluntary.

Iris Marion Young has criticised the ideal of community and her comments have purchase here. Community, she says, relies on identity and presence and on a certain relation to those whom we feel to be the same as us (Young 1990). Located within a critique of self/other relations grounded in sameness, this is clearly a problematic foundation for affinity. The danger here is that difference will be subordinated in favour of sameness. We will like those to whom we are alike. Friendship, in this critique, has its own baggage and is not an appropriate grounding for sustainable self/other relations. Private likes and dislikes should not ground public civility. Young's preference is for an ideal(ised) city in which difference and heterogeneity are possible and welcome. Small face-to-face communities will, she fears, suppress difference.

Nonetheless, at the level of motivation, the need for 'community' is a key factor in intentional communities. People seek a community that offers an intimacy that they do not find in 'mainstream' society.

I hate to admit this but a few years ago I was walking up a street with a friend of mine (Digger), when an old woman fell over. He went to help her and I carried on walking as if nothing had happened because I was worried someone would see me doing this ... I am glad to say I learnt my lesson when I thought about this. I was impressed with Digger for helping her.

(Shaun, PIC, 23 November 1997)

A sense of community and responsibility and relationship with other people ... community spirit. I think this is a major factor which the local towns lost for a while but is slowly returning through credit unions and other organisations.

(Shaun, PIC, 27 November 1997)

If the end result of high capitalist society is alienation, social deprivation and a (classless?) impoverished culture – as the rhetoric of contemporary British politics would have it – then communities may belong to part of a grassroots emergent alternative. A bloc of opposition, perhaps?

Internal meets external

Conceptual meeting spaces

I have, thus far, assumed the division of public and private to be 'the' main, major, dominant, way in which the public/private relation has been conceived of in the liberal tradition. Liberal thought and values I take to be integral to the culture and values of contemporary British society. If separation underpins the relation of public and private and this equates to a devaluing of the private then my tactic (of re-valuing the private and arguing that it can be political) might enable us to think usefully about two spheres of life without de-politicising either. So far, so good. There have, however, 'always' (by which I mean, since the early days of Christianity, and certainly throughout the history of liberal thought) been moments of transgression of this binary, this separation of public and private.

One space in which this gap is bridged is that in which private relationships and events are publicly celebrated through ritual. Daily service, communion and all manner of religious ceremonies are a public 'sharing' of private faith, but I am thinking particularly of those ceremonies with which we mark events of private significance. The wedding, for instance: deeply complex and the subject of much analysis; is, even at the most superficial glance, the public celebration of the sexual bonding of two people. Marriage is many things: a joining, a pledge, a contract, a religious institution, a social and economic institution, a legal contract, an act of personal commitment, a context in which legitimately to engender [*sic*] and rear children. Etymologically linked to *maritus*: husband, it has a history of property relations and associations which feminist analysts find somewhat problematic. It is not my role here to explore this terrain. Some (few) community members whom I interviewed were married, but that also is not why

I raise this. My interest is in the fact that weddings (secular and religious), funerals, barmitzvahs, christenings, all are moments at which private becomes public. They are a subversion of the separation of public and private.

Though these moments are transgressive of the separation of public and private, they are not, I suggest, times of significant transgression in political terms. On the contrary, they are times at which cultural, political and economic conformities are inscribed onto private moments. They allow public culture and institutions to name and in some way control private events and relationships.

At each of these times a number of significant things occur:

- Approbation. These are times at which public approval (blessing) is given to events, occasions and relationships. They are moments of acceptance.
- Initiation. They celebrate something intimate and private through rites of passage (conjugal, nuptial and burial). They are moments of movement into a community within the wider community.
- Regularisation. The event or relationship becomes identifiable. Each and every partnership is, for instance, different, but marriage provides a contract and a set of expectations within which the relationship is then contextualised. It is a codification: an inscription of a set of rules and codes of behaviour onto a given partnership.
- Professionalisation. Ritualisation of these events, and the fact that this, following a prescribed order of proceedings, involves professionals: priests, registrars, musicians, caterers. These ceremonies have economic as well as cultural significance. Often the 'performers' of the ritual have high social status; they are 'professional'.

Increasingly, these ceremonies become secularised and some people in intentional communities are concerned with the process of taking ownership of ritual. This is interesting and warrants further research. For now though I offer this as another gesture towards the creation of transgressive inversions and subversions of deeply conservative codifying phenomenon. At Talamh, Angela told me about the community's involvement in the home birth of her daughter. There was a real sense of occasion and shared ownership of the moment. Others, for example, Chris and his partner at PIC work with groups that publicly invent rituals (The Welfare State Group's *Dead Good Funeral Book*, e.g., aims to educate and empower people to make decisions about how they really want to be buried.) At Findhorn the full moon is greeted, and indigenous shamanism and paganism filter into many dances and celebrations in community events and celebrations. It seems to me interesting that people in intentional communities should in some way be thinking about ways to inscribe their own culture onto these moments of public–private significance. Perhaps these are times at which such a thing is most possible – places of transgression in which a new utopian consciousness can be articulated.

Internal meets external

Blocs of opposition?

Of course, one way of reading all of this would be to view it as an emergence of a cultural or social phenomena: interesting, but not of political relevance. This would, I think, be to miss something exciting. For one thing, with the possible exception of Findhorn, ecologically informed intentional communities in the UK engage also in politics in the more conventional sense of the term. They are politicised spaces. They are, mostly, busy in terms that would normally be named political activity. Briefly, they offer to some a temporary resting place between engagement in direct action and eco-politics and often members have a (continuing) history of political activism. Janie and Ali at Talamh, for instance, had lived at the Pollock Free State. This formed part of popular protest into the building of the M77 link motorway in Ayrshire. Protest began in 1978, but a public enquiry in 1988 gave the road the go-ahead. In 1994 Stop the Ayr Road Route Alliance (STARR) was launched. It comprised twenty local and environmental organisations. The Free State was established in 1994. It had 1,000 passport-holding citizens and a core of ten to thirty residents. Even after the 'failure' of the campaign, the Free State remains an icon of resistance, a veritable space of transgression and utopian creativity.

> The Pollock Free State played a dual function. Firstly, it was primarily oriented towards oppositional *resistance* ... Its secondary function was to offer positive cultural *alternatives* to [the] dominant hegemony.
>
> (Seel 1997a: 3)

Gaia, at Earthworm, has a history with the Rainbow Tribe. The Rainbow Tribe was housed at the One World Rainbow Centre in Kentish Town, which is self-described as 'an environmental community centre providing space for a wide range of positive and creative projects. We set up following the Rio Earth Summit in 1992 as a DIY grassroots by-the-people-for-the-people initiative' (Rainbow Tribe, 1995, 'Short guide'). The Rainbow Tribe was composed of squatters and homeless volunteers, committed to non-violent direct local action, and had environmental aims:

> To create a space where people from all races, cultures and walks of life can come together to effect positive change. The Rainbow Tribe/Collective is part of a grassroots movement across the country and around the world. The growth of our movement depends on continually making connections with groups and individuals. We are building a loving global community to live in harmony with the earth, by interlinking, communicating, and weaving the web of life together.
>
> (*ibid.*)

The Tribe forge active links with a multitude of organisations, ranging from Earth First! and other direct-action groups (hunt saboteurs, free information network) to intentional communities, lobby groups and housing charities: over fifty associated organisations are listed on their publicity material.

Intentional communities offer physical space for political gatherings, festivals and events: in 1997, for instance, Talamh hosted the annual gathering of Earth First! Alex describes this radical ecological movement here:

> Earth First! is seeking a paradigm shift from a multi-issue perspective. Our strategy is one of rapid response. We are able to move very fast due to the nature of our organisation, it works because we have a non-hierarchical structure. Our two slogans are 'No Compromise' and 'By Any Means'.
>
> (Alex, unpublished paper given at the Direct Action and British Environmentalism Conference, 15 October 1997, at Keele University)

At Earthworm, there is a space offered for campers and events called the Peacefield. It is part of the International Peace Garden, described here by Sue: 'it's bits of forest planted all over the world together with the same name – they are all interconnected' (6 September 1998). In 1997 this space was used to host a gathering of the UK Animal Liberation Front. Gaia: 'showing we support them is showing people we're a political group' (6 September 1997).

Members of intentional communities work with local pressure groups and political groups: many work with the local Agenda 21 initiative that emerged from the 1992 UN Earth Summit. This aims to contribute to a commitment made at that summit to the creation of a blueprint for social and economic development in the twenty-first century. It is based on what it states to be the realisation that 'we cannot have a healthy society or economy in a world with so much poverty and destruction' (Local Agenda 21 leaflet), and acknowledges the need for major changes in attitudes and lifestyles.

They represent spaces from which individuals can go out and work and play in external political spaces. I cited Chris above, talking about 'nice place to live' syndrome. The conversation continued thus:

> Also though, they are a resource – it's a question of what you use those resources for – as a way of participating politically, or as just, 'Well, this is nice – sit back and do nothing'.
>
> (Chris, PIC, 12 December 1997)

At People In Common (PIC), Mike works in a socialist library. Paul works as a tutor for people with learning difficulties with a community charity called Jigsaw. Chris runs Green Build, which is an ecological building company. He also has links with the Welfare State theatre group. Shaun is a youth worker. Derek and several others run the workers' co-operative.

Intentional communities are often the homes of alternative industry and business. At PIC there is the hardwood centre, which is a workers' co-operative. At Blackcurrant, Drew runs a Box Scheme, which allows local people access to affordable organic fruit and vegetables. An entire network of peripheral New Age businesses exists around the Findhorn Foundation. These were mentioned in Chapter 1, and include alternative and complementary health services – masseuses, therapists, shiatsu practitioners, herbalists and apothecaries, as well as ecological building companies, and clothes designers, craftspeople and artists. Some of these are workers' co-operatives. Some, such as 'EarthShare', involve people from the wider community as well as members of the Foundation.

Tom Moylan, writing in 1986, offered an optimistic reading of fictional utopias as critical in what he called a 'nuclear' sense. They are, he suggests, part of a historic bloc of opposition to capitalism. This bloc consists of socialist, feminist and ecological elements. There is evidence in the brief survey above that intentional communities are part of a larger – albeit diffuse – movement of political opposition. In this they may contribute, on a small scale, to a critical mass that can have a transformative effect. PIC, for instance, is one of the older communities included in this book. It has, over time, established links and had influence in both the world of communes and its local community. Chris, one of the early members of the community, told me how their workers' co-operative has slowly gained a reputation amongst the traditional co-operative movement. When they first started going to meetings of CRS (Co-operative Retail Stores), they were greeted with some suspicion. This was returned as PIC members felt the politics of the local communist party to be corrupt at that time. Over time though relations have been established as mutually respectful. Similarly, Derek, who still works in the Hardwood Centre, recounts the slow process of establishing for themselves a reputation as serious businesspeople, with a quality product to market. Local counsellors in the area have consulted the community about alternative housing arrangements and are currently exploring tenant-ownership schemes.

Chris, at PIC, is one of the editors of *Diggers and Dreamers: A Guide to Co-operative Living*. This is an annual publication that has become the bible of potential members. Its role might be said to be also one of demonstration, although the audience is different.

> Entrepreneurs make money by taking risks and what we've been doing is being social entrepreneurs. It's an experiment in democratic living that maybe others can learn from – our mistakes as well as our successes.
>
> (Chris, PIC, 12 December 1997)

Conclusions

The being and doing and study of politics

If, as the liberal canon would have it, the individual is separate (ontologically, spatially, conceptually) from the state, and if the state is where 'politics'

happens; if the actions, thoughts and deeds of the 'private' individual are not of political concern; if this individual needs protection and shelter from the state in order to retain his [*sic*] privacy and self-sovereignty, if, if, if ... ad infinitum ... then the public and the private clearly and unproblematically can be assumed to be separate and a legitimate conceptual dualism: a useful tool of analysis.

However, it is my contention that transgressions of the public/private divide help us to problematise the separation (conceptual and cultural) of the personal and the political. Thus we are able to perceive – feel, observe, experience – that these separations are contextual and located in a specific tradition and history. The separation of the public from the private is not a phenomenon on which we can found a universalist politics. If composting domestic sewage, deciding where to live, using your home as a space of political opposition and creativity, using your home to host political gatherings and events, using your home as a showcase for inspiration – if these and the other activities mentioned in this chapter are, as I have suggested, political activities, then we are witnessing a radical politicisation of private space.

This touches on questions of citizenship and agency. Our understanding of the public and the private: their meaning, significance and relationship, informs our understanding of a number of key political concepts. One such is citizenship, which is, in turn, connected to political and moral agency and political identity. Theories of citizenship invariably include some reference to political activity. In other words, citizens participate in political life. If these people are indeed acting as agents of political change, then they can, perhaps, be considered to be part of a mass of critical opposition (Moylan 1986: 11). I have indicated some of the extent and scope of the networks of which intentional communities form a part. Similarly, if these activities are considered to be political, then these political agents might be reconceived of as active citizens, rather than as slothful dropouts. One certain thing, even from such a brief analysis as that undertaken in this chapter, is that much is occurring in the world of radical environmental politics. Much of this occurs out of the range of the public eye. Because they occur in the domestic and private sphere, the nature of these actions are not noticed. They are thus trivial, irrelevant and not political. Of course, there is much activity that is in the eyes of the media and the public, but to see the 'actions', the protests and the stunts, is to see only the tip of the iceberg. Consciousness and awareness of the scope of the transgressive political action of intentional communities might contribute to the paradigm shift in consciousness necessary for sustainable political change.

Intentional communities re-invent the political, even within the parameters of their own political culture. An example of this comes from Talamh. I mentioned earlier that an Earth First! gathering was held there in 1997. Earth First! is an innovative movement. It makes exciting moves in the re-invention of the political and is part of the radicalised political environmental politics in Britain today. Talamh is located between two large open-cast mines – their presence as an oasis of ecologically sound practice in this space is both ironic and intentional.

Given their infamy as monkeywrenchers and eco-warriors, Earth First!'s decision to engage in an 'action' as a part of the gathering was anticipated by the state authorities and the place was crawling with police and cameramen. The action was to be against the mining practices. With conscious irony and humour, the Earth Firsters picked up hoes and garden forks and picks and set off: dreadlocks flying in the wind ... for the local primary school, where they spent the afternoon working on a permaculture garden. Wonderful and refreshing, this kind of thing breathes some fresh clean air back into our thinking on politics.

4 Property

The first man who, having enclosed a piece of land, thought of saying 'this is mine' and found people simple enough to believe him, was the true founder of civil society. How many crimes, wars, murders; how much misery and horror the human race would have been spared if someone had pulled up the stakes and filled in the ditch and cried out to his fellow men: 'Beware of listening to this imposter. You are lost if you forget that the fruits of this earth belong to everyone and that the earth itself belongs to no one!'

(Jean-Jacques Rousseau, *Discourse on the Origin of Inequality*, Part 2)

Introduction

Property is at once central and marginal to political theory. It is central in that the consideration of most political concepts: power, equality, freedom, justice, involves – to some degree – consideration of the concept of property and its attendants (ownership, money, possessions and work). It is marginal in that, in itself, it is a neglected topic of study. The communities that form the basis of this project do not own their property in conventional ways; they are, in this, marginal. I hope to draw from the discussions that follow an account that might be of value to the broader community of scholarship and ownership of property. From the margins then I hope to draw something of interest to the centre.

Approaches to property come in a variety of forms. Secondary commentators predictably identify a number of discipline-driven approaches (Reeve 1986; Hollowell 1982). These are described variously as the psychological, the legal, the political, the philosophical and the economic approaches. Whilst these labels no doubt have some currency, in that different disciplines have different agendum, standards and expectations of scholarship, and are thereby likely to ask different questions of a topic, I shall not employ them here. The differences within disciplines are too great and the differences between them too small to make this a useful way of separating different accounts of property.

Another common approach in the secondary literature is to focus on individual thinkers (Macpherson 1978; Ryan 1987). These accounts have merit and some contribute valuable insights beyond that of textbook surveys. An example is C. B. Macpherson's concept of possessive individualism (1978). Other, more complex, approaches include those that tease out what is argued to be a central problematic in the concept of property. Examples are work on the justification of ownership (Grunnebaum 1987); and a preoccupation with rights (Waldron 1988); The identification and thorough interrogation of a central paradox or problem in the concept of property is a valuable exercise, but is not my aim here.

In this chapter, I shall attempt to combine attention to the scope offered by the broad-sweeping accounts and the attention paid to the particular in these latter conceptually focused explorations, whilst also referring to contributions from disciplines external to the study of politics. Primarily though, my discussion takes its lead from the transcripts of my interviews with people who live in intentional communities. The bodies of thought to which this chapter refers are feminism, deep ecology, deconstrucive theory and the utopian canon. The utopian tradition, in particular, has not yet been thoroughly mined for its contribution to property debates – notwithstanding Peter Beilhartz's contribution (Beilhartz 1992). I shall attempt in some way to remedy this by referral to primary texts of utopian imagining from thinkers such as Plato, Thomas More and William Morris.

The central question with which I began research for this chapter is this: What, if anything, can be learned from a short study of alternative property relations, as lived in intentional communities? I shall suggest that intentional communities are spaces in which transgression and utopianism can be explored and further that these communities offer pragmatic and practical examples of alternative property relations from which many interesting theoretical questions can be pursued.

The communities: ownership

The properties

A fuller description of these communities is available in Chapter 1. Briefly though:

Findhorn

The physical space occupied by the Findhorn Foundation is on two sites in Morayshire. One, Cluny Hill College, is in the town of Forres, the other, The Park, is near the village of Findhorn a few miles distant. Cluny consists of one impressive building: a former hotel set in gardens. It houses over a hundred people and is the main centre for educational workshops and courses. Cluny belongs to Findhorn Foundation. The Park was originally a caravan site but now has a fair number of semi-permanent and permanent structures of various types. These buildings range from pre-fabs to houses made of recycled whiskey barrels to a straw-bale structure, and various ecologically experimental homes. There is also a new area: 'The Field of Dreams', on which building plots are available at the time of writing. This will be an eco-village. Many of the homes at The Park are privately owned, though their sale is mediated by the Foundation, and so they are not available on the open market.

> On a descriptive level, The Foundation is split between two sites. It's clear that the lifestyle here at Cluny is very different from that lifestyle at The Park. It's different, I mean – we're all part of the same community, but you could say that Cluny itself could be regarded as a self-contained community.
>
> (Patrick, Findhorn, 3 January 1998)

Erraid

Erraid is a small tidal island of 1 square mile, which lies by Mull off the West Coast of Scotland. The island is owned by a Dutch family. The community are the island's caretakers. The family has access to the island and take possession of it for 2 months each summer. In terms of ownership then it is a simple case of privately owned land, which has an intentional community as its caretakers.

Clearly, the nature of the relationship between the owners of Erraid and its caretakers has an impact on the ability of the community to fulfil its own mission or vision. The fact that the community on Erraid does not have fully legal autonomy causes certain practical restrictions. Peter spoke of

> The paradoxes of this place. The Dutch ownership. The nature of trying to do things in a self-sufficient way needs people with a long view – if people are not here that long it's an in-built paradox.
>
> (Peter, Erraid, 28 August 1997)

However, this is seen also as a virtuous contingency, in that it facilitates a space of co-operation:

> The other side of things here is that we're caretakers of the island for the Dutch. So we work within their vision of the place, which is conservation. Also, we share the island with other people – the guests who come here.
>
> (Elizabeth, Erraid, 26 August 1997)

Beech Hill

Beech Hill is a large house in Devon with extensive gardens.

> There's seven acres of land, a big old house, a stable block that's converted into cottages, lots of people living in the house, people living in the cottages, a large Victorian walled garden with lots of vegetables growing in it, a

paddock for camping and for animals to stay in – although we haven't got any animals that we keep there – a swimming pool, a small vineyard, a workshop. . . .

(Amanda, Beech Hill, 13 September 1997)

Blackcurrant

Blackcurrant is an urban housing co-operative. It owns two houses in Northampton. One is rented out, and the other is home to the eight co-op members.

We're in the larger of the two houses, which has space for probably 8 or 9 people and is currently housing 7 adults and 3 children. We've got lots of workshop space; we've got some garden space. The house is about 100 years old. We work hard to maintain it and try to build it up – it looks like a normal house, you wouldn't know it was a community house.

(Dru, Blackcurrant, 2 July 1997)

Talamh

The house at Talamh is a medieval-century farmhouse, and the co-op also owns the surrounding 50 acres of land. It is in Lanarkshire, near the M74 between two open-cast mines.

Talamh is a sixteenth century farmhouse, it's got fifty acres of land and there are 14 people here at present, two babies and another one on the way and we are five years old. It was set up originally by five founder members.

(Janie, Talamh, 9 August 1997)

People in Common

People in Common now live in a former corn mill on the banks of the Lancashire Calder. This co-op started life in Burnley in several separate houses but is now based at the Mill, which its members have converted to living accommodation, and the 5-acre garden. At my first visit, PIC had eight adult members.

Well, we started off mostly as people who'd been involved in squatting and looking for a way of housing ourselves in better ways. ... We originally agreed to look for a way to live together near a town ... we've been pretty much a housing co-operative. A housing co-operative that has one actual house where people ate together; a small commune where we lived and ate in the same house; and now a bit more of a diffuse shared house with some communal parts in it, rather than a whole commune.

(Derek, People in Common, 7 December 1997)

Earthworm

Earthworm, in Shropshire, was formerly a large family house with 7 acres of land.

> It's a big rambling house, it needs quite a lot of work on it really and especially the roof. The communal areas downstairs are vegan. We've got seven and a half acres of land, I'm not sure how much of it is International Peacefield, but there are fields at the back and quite a lot of garden.
>
> (Sue, Earthworm, 6 September 1998)

How property is owned

Mixed ownership

Most of Britain's ecological intentional communities are co-operatively owned. The exceptions are those connected with The Findhorn Foundation, to which I shall turn in a minute, and Beech Hill. This community has a mixed ownership, some private and some held by trustees. In legal terms it is a Company Limited by Guarantee, which is managed by its trustees. This community is recovering from serious and threatening financial crisis. It was formerly possessed by means of a mixture of fully mutual and private ownership.

> The community now feels like a different sort of community to the one I came to because we've been through an awful lot of changes. ... The community I came to was more clear-cut, partly because there was somebody here at the time who controlled things in a way, which didn't really feel good – on the other hand it helped how it was run. ... We just didn't know how financially unstable this thing was ... we didn't realise what this chap had done, he was doing his best, but we had to ask him to stand down and then figure out what was going on. We were paying so much interest on the interest that was owing to the bank that our accountant advised us to go insolvent and then it was hard because there was quite a shock for us because myself amongst others had put all our savings in and I lost £10,000 – others lost double that.
>
> (Dawn, Beech Hill, 13 September 1997)

The history of Beech Hill shows that living in community is not an easy or guaranteed route to a nice home.

Co-operative ownership

> You are both tenant and landlord, but you own the thing without actually owning it. It's non-possessive ownership. You leave the thing behind when you go. In the Primary Rules of the co-op, which are registered with The

Friendly Society, you can't sell a co-op property for personal profit. So I can't just sell my share of The Mill. We, as a collective, could sell The Mill, but we'd have to reinvest the money from the sale in something used for similar purposes – common good. We're more guardians than owners; we're guardians of the co-operative, not owners.

Usually when you own something you have to buy it. You're given it, or you inherit it, or you exchange money with value for it and you possess it. With a fully mutual you don't have to do this. You don't 'buy in' to a fully mutual. Owning usually involves buying, but with this you're given a share. We 'pay' £1 to join the co-op and that gives us limited liability. . . . This is so that if, say, we go bankrupt, then on insolvency, if we're found to have behaved in an unsavoury way, against the rules of the co-op, then we're liable. If we've acted according to the rules and the insolvency is because of something like market forces, then we are protected by the limited liability. It's a way of protecting the innocent, but getting the bad 'uns. . . . Yes, it's just. In a society where justice is usually for the property owners.

(Paul, PIC, 1 October 1998)

I shall return again to this quote, as it is rich to interpret, for now though it provides a useful introduction to the mechanics of co-operative ownership. A co-op is, then, a Limited Company, registered with the Register of Friendly Societies. Co-op records are subject to scrutiny and inspection. Routes to membership vary from community to community, but generally involve a number of initial visits, followed by a period of trial membership, and invitation by consensus. Co-ops are bound by their own rules (Pierson 1995). Here, by way of example of these key points, is a section from the rules of Blackcurrant.[1]

We have a set of rules – primary and secondary – the secondary rules are not really ready for writing down as they are in the process of change. They include more philosophical aims of the co-op's members and so may include a policy on ethical consumption and levels of income.

(Dru, Blackcurrant, 7 October 1998)

Paul's comment about not actually buying a share in the Co-op is probably worth unpacking. It is apparent also from Blackcurrant's rules that shares are not, strictly speaking, 'owned'. They are not sold on: the £1 is not refundable upon leaving the Co-op but is rather surrendered. This is not an exchange in any reciprocal or regular sense. Two things are striking about this form of ownership: first that the 'value' of the share is disproportionate to the 'cost' of the share: all that for £1! Second, membership and consequent

---

1 See Appendix A for the full Rules of this co-op.

Name, objects, registered office

2   The objects of the Co-operative shall be:

a   the construction, conversion, improvement and management on the co-operative principle of the dwellings for occupation by members of the Co-operative under an agreement to occupy ... granted to them by the Co-operative.

b   The provision and improvement on the co-operative principle of land or buildings for purposes connected with the requirements of the members occupying the houses provided or managed by the Co-operative.

4   The Co-operative shall not trade for profit.

Share capital

6

a   The share capital of the Co-operative shall consist of shares of the nominal value of One Pound each issued to the members of the Co-operative upon admission to membership.

b   Shares shall be neither withdrawable nor transferable, shall carry no right to interest, dividend or bonus and shall be forfeited and cancelled on cessation of membership from whatever cause and the amount paid thereon shall become the property of the Membership.

Membership

7

a   The members of the Co-operative shall be persons whose names are entered on the register of members.

b   Only tenants and prospective tenants are eligible to become members.

c   A member shall hold one share only in the Co-operative.

---

ownership is not so much a financial exchange as a symbol of social inclusion – in addition to being a hard-nosed pragmatic legal contract of ownership.

Concepts of ownership

Connected to these ways of legally owning physical property is a way of thinking about property and ownership, which I should now like to explore. Two phrases from Paul's description above have particular resonance here:

> It's non-possessive ownership.
> We're more guardians than owners.[2]

These ideas of guarding, protecting and being responsible for place were variously articulated in all of the communities visited. This is not to say that each expression of guardianship came from the same political or ideological perspective. Some were clearly talking about what might be called 'green' holistic approaches to the external environment. Others came from a socialist standpoint and still others were self-described as anarchist.

Green political thought is interesting on this as it stresses the importance of connection between people and place. Jonathan Porritt, for instance, writes of agriculture, which he says

> binds people to the natural processes of the Earth and, with the use of appro-
> priate technology, creates a sense of harmony that is sorely lacking.
>
> (Porritt in Dobson 1995: 115)

Deep ecology theory takes the concept of custodianship and draws from it a view of the Good Life. Further, it is part of the paradigm shift in consciousness desired by some political ecologists in order to realise their vision of a sustainable society. An ethic of responsibility is at the heart of many green visions of the ideal polity. An example is the blueprint gestured by Kirkpatrick Sale, whose bioregionalism takes as its normative starting point the belief that:

> We must see that living with the land means living in, and according to the
> ways and rhythms of its natural regions – its bioregions.
>
> (Sale 1985: 56)

Often commentators use this view of relation to the earth as a way of distinguishing deep ecology from light green environmentalism (Eckersley 1992; Naess 1973; Dobson 1990). For David Pepper, this view is part of what he calls 'First Order Ecocentric Principles':

> Holism – interdependence with nature. Humans as part of natural systems,
> not divorced from them. A harmonious relationship of stewardship is
> required. (Pepper 1991: 227)

---

2 This description came from a recorded conversation with Paul, during which I asked him to describe co-operative ownership. In my initial interviews property ownership was not part of my questions, yet the sentiments and terms expressed here re-occur in the transcripts.

Stewardship is a term that was volunteered in several interviews. Patrick links it here to a love of place not dissimilar to the love one might feel for a dependent person.

> I suppose I've got a sense of custodianship of the place, I love it. I've always lived at Cluny. I feel like a guardian of the place, a steward or something and I, yeah, I'm just glad to be a part of it, to put something into the place.
>
> (Patrick, Findhorn, 3 January 1998)

For deep ecologists, ecological politics is about preserving the planet rather than advantaging humanity (Kemp and Wall, 1990: 11). An ecocentric view of the world imposes upon humans a responsibility of care. The source or grounding of this responsibility is not drawn from reciprocity, or contract, or from mutually binding duties. These are at the root of much (human) rights discourse. The earth is not an agent in the sense assumed by rights theses. It cannot 'contract', nor can it offer reciprocity. Rather, in much green philosophy it is simply a given Other. By this is meant that it is something ontologically and empirically prior to ourselves, to whom we owe automatic responsibility. This non-reciprocal responsibility is illustrative of what I have referred to elsewhere as a paradigm shift in the way that we think.

Intentional communities are not the only places where such shifts can occur. They are, however, good places for such thinking to flourish and be explored. I shall expand on this further in the next chapter in my discussion of Self/Other relations. For now, it is sufficient to note the different conceptions of ownership and possession that arise from deep ecology. I am, however, wary of suggesting that the statements of custodianship by communards are articulations of a particular worldview. This would be an inappropriate claim. There is diversity between and amongst communities, and the people with whom I spoke were not, on the whole, claiming to act as spokespeople for one ideological worldview. What can be safely claimed is that the stewardship mentioned here by the practical 'diggers' and the utopian 'dreamers' are views of ownership which differ from a simple 'this is mine and I therefore look after it'.

This latter view is at the core of much liberal political thought and, I think, lies at the heart of liberal democratic property law (Waldron 1998). The notion is the original property of John Locke. Locke's theory of property is manifestly straightforward: he imagines a pre-political state (the State of Nature). This is a world prior to government and legislation. He asks: 'What are just laws?' and: 'How did they come to be so?' His response is couched in rhetoric of ownership. Just law, for Locke, protects the individual's private property. The ownership of property in this State of Nature comes from Man's (God-given) sovereignty over his own person: from ownership of the self. In a peculiar move, much commented on ever since, Locke extends this original property over one's own person to his goods and possessions.

Though the Earth, and all inferior Creatures be common to all Men, yet every Man has a *Property* in his own *Person*. . . . The *Labour* of his Body, and the *Work* of his Hands, we may say, are properly his. Whatsoever then he removes out of the State that Nature hath provided, and left it in, he hath mixed his *Labour* with and joyned to it something that is his own, and thereby makes it his *Property*.

(Locke, Book IV: 27 in Laslett 1964)

In the State of Nature property is legitimately acquired thus: mixing one's labour (which we all own) with something external to the self that is part of the common store makes it proper to the self: property. Property in this conception is 'of the self', pertaining to the self: proper to the self. This is discussed further in Chapter 5.

There arises from this a view that ownership is a permissive state. If I own something in the same way that I own myself, I have a right of some kind to dispose of it or exchange it or treat it as my will and reason dictate. For Locke though, waste and surplus limited the right to possession in a pre-money economy:

Whatsoever he tilled and reaped, laid up and made use of, before it spoiled, that was his peculiar Right; whatsoever he enclosed, and could feed, and make use of, the Cattle and the Product was also his. But if either the Grass of his enclosure rotted on the ground, or the Fruit of his planting perished without gathering, and laying up, this part of the Earth, notwithstanding his Inclosure, was still to be looked on as Waste, and might be the possessions of any other.

(*ibid.*, Book IV: 38)

The following statement comes from Mike at PIC. He is describing land use and value. There is, at first glance, some similarity between Mike's account and the classically liberal view that was the prodigy of Locke's Treatise.

from my point of view, we have here a resource, we're diggers, we hold the land in, what do you call it – we look after it: we're custodians. I mean that's the word I feel about this place. We don't have the right to five acres of land like this without using it in some kind of way, that means that other people, the broader community, have as much right to it as we do.

(Mike, PIC, 20 September 1997)

Mike evokes utility as grounds for ownership. The big difference here is that, for Locke, utility and waste become irrelevant once money comes to symbolically represent surplus in the economy. Mike later talked about his belief that the land and possessions should be shared with the wider community and of a responsibility to use such things in some socially valuable way. Rightful land ownership, in this account, is linked to social good. I mention Mike at this point because there is nothing particularly 'green' about his account. To a certain extent it matters not whence the ideas lie in the rainbow or spectrum of ideologies. The point of real interest here is in the fact that people who live in communities where land ownership is different to the normal model of private ownership have some account of this, which is, in some way, transgressive of dominant understandings.

The people on Erraid all spoke of custodianship. In literal terms, of course, this is hardly remarkable, given their relationship with the owners. However, the sense of connection between people and place that they express goes beyond a legal relationship to something more complex and personal:

> [When I first came here] the island was like a lover for me. I would go to the island and I would get everything from the island, it was like – it just gave me so much. It was a real relationship, you know. Every Sunday I'd be off to just go all around the edge, exploring every nook and cranny. . . . I'm so glad I had that time, before getting involved in a human relationship because an intimate knowledge is good.
>
> (Katie, Erraid, 28 July 1997)

Katie speaks from within the heart of the New Age Movement and for her the connection with land is articulated in terms of a spiritual (and embodied) relation. Not everyone in this community agreed to a formal interview but at some time or other during my stay on Erraid, each member of this small community spoke of a bond to place. Katie's description of her early 'relationship' with Erraid serves to illustrate a sense of connectedness to place.

Of course, many people love where they live. And Erraid is wild and beautiful; it is a breathtaking place. Likewise many feel a sense of custodianship – farmers often articulate their connection to the land in this way, as do gardeners (see Paul and Mike above). This feeling is not the exclusive 'property' of either intentional communities generally or the particular perspective of this community. However, it is, I think, worthy of note that people in intentional communities tend to have a strong sense of connection to their homes which is often unrelated to individual gain or to private ownership. Rather, there is, in the interview transcripts, a strong and recurrent sense of people belonging to a place, rather than *vice versa*. This is not, in most cases, due to local affinity or heritage. Most community dwellers are mobile in this way. Further, there is a corresponding sense of custodianship, privilege and responsibility.

Work

Work is central to the identity of many communities. In some, it is an expression of individuality within the collective. In others it forms the bond that binds people together. In all cases work for the community is part of something different to the everyday external context. Work tends usually, in the wider community, to be part of a property economy: we work generally for money. In most cases work occurred both within and externally to the intentional community. I shall begin with the exceptions.

At Erraid, all work is internal to the community. Nobody earns a wage from outside the community's enclosed economic system. Erraid aims to be self-sustaining in fresh produce. Fruit and vegetables are grown on site, and dairy products are gleaned from their two cows. This presents an obvious challenge given their physical context: a small island on the West Coast of Scotland, and it requires vast amounts of labour. Visitors and hosts work together with the common aim of sustaining life. It is a labour-intensive system. At meal times, even in the relatively balmy summer months, one is acutely aware of the amount of labour that has been given to each meal. Each community member has responsibility for a given area of work (examples include herb garden, vegetable garden, candle workshop). Guests work alongside members and are invited to 'attune': to think about the tasks that they feel able and willing to help with. The work is varied and mostly unskilled. During a week there in the summer of 1997, I worked with other guests and dug holes for gateposts and erected a gate and fence. Another day I spent polishing candles and I had several stints at the endless weeding. Others worked on compost, cut wood and cooked.

The pattern of work at the Findhorn Foundation is similar. The level of involvement depends on the guest's status: people attending workshops do not generally get involved in the working life of the community but others do. For instance, work forms a large part of other programmes such as Experience Week, Living in Community Guest and the Student Year Programme. The choices of work available are usually between working in one of the three gardens or the two kitchens, or the dining room, or 'homecare' (domestic care of The Park and Cluny). From the point of view of the guests, work is an important part of a stay at Findhorn. By working alongside community members, labour and craft are experienced in ways somehow different to waged work 'on the outside'.

The connection between work and wage is severed at all Findhorn Foundation communities (Newbold House, Forres, Cluny, The Park and Erraid). Membership of the Findhorn Foundation comes in varies forms, according to length of connection and depth of involvement. In all cases that I encountered though, work was not paid according to conventional value of labour. The 120 or so full members of the Foundation receive an allowance, which is 'about enough to run a car on' (Patrick, Cluny, 4 January 1997). Some members of the Open Community, who are people who live locally (sometimes on site), work for an hourly rate of approximately £5 (in 1997). People who live locally but are not connected to the Foundation are incredulous about this aspect in particular: Guests pay and then work for free? Members don't get salaries? People who work in the offices don't get paid more than those who labour in the gardens do?

Foundation members account for this by reference to the religious concept of service.

[Of the work] It's like, for me, finding the connection with the hand, it's so much more than tapping the keyboard or using the telephone. It's really life and the feet also – carrying forward. So I just find that incredibly enabling and because the tasks are simple anyone can come at any level of skill and they'll still be useful, and I find that, for me, one of the great gifts of Erraid is being able to give and to give of myself and to serve the island and the people who come.

(Katie, Erraid, 28 July 1997)

Katie follows this with a caveat:

I know when I say 'serve' that it's a word I shrank from before [earlier in the interview] but it's like I feel incredibly blessed to have the privilege to work and be here and work and be part of that and, you know, people come here with all sorts of things to work through.

(Katie, Erraid, 28 July 1997)

Earlier in the interview she had explained the relationship between guest and member by saying:

It wouldn't work for us to be serving our paying guests as if we were their sort of support system or paid servants or whatever.

(Katie, Erraid, 28 July 1997)

The kind of service to which Katie refers is clearly not that offered by a hotel or 'service' industry. As was mentioned in Chapter 2, Erraid's external revenue comes from two sources: the visitors and the sale of the candles produced in the small workshop. Guests are the main source of income. They are channelled mostly from Findhorn, but some come also through external advertising or word of mouth because they are interested in the ecological lifestyle, and/or the fact that this is a spiritual community. Many return. The system of payment is interesting. A guide price is advertised. This consists of a scale from approximately £40 to £280. At the end of the week, guests are invited to think about how much they want to offer. This is not a materially rich community, life is hard and possessions are minimal. Although the islanders are dependent on guests for a large portion of their income, the relationship between them is articulated in such a way as to avoid relations of 'consumer' and 'provider', or 'customer' and 'supplier'. Rather the content of the service offered is couched in terms of facilitation: a stay on the island is an opportunity to sort yourself out, to tune into nature, to experience spiritual community, etc. Guests make of the stay what they will.

Service in the sense of a gift of labour – as described by Katie – has its roots in religious tradition. The account is constructed as one of dignified submission to something that exceeds the self. This interpretation would not, I think, be antithetical to the Findhorn account of itself as found in publicity literature: 'Work is Love in Action' is, for instance, a slogan that frequently recurs in pamphlets and on the web site. Though money is an essential part of this, the relationship described by Katie is not primarily economic. Indeed, in terms of efficiency and cost, the food production on Erraid and at Findhorn is so labour intensive as to be uneconomic in financial terms. Adding the labour hours and their market value would surely make the food produced so expensive as to make a straight-forward financial exchange relation more cheap: why not just take paying guests and feed them on purchased food whilst taking a salary from the income? That is not what these communities are about. Without wishing to particularly endorse these systems, I should like to suggest that they do represent some fairly complex paradigm shifts on consciousness regarding work, labour and value.

> Part of the underpinning of the community is to do with service and discovering spirit through service and that seems to be my way.
>
> (Patrick, Findhorn, 4 January 1998)

> It's a place to work and serve and grow.
>
> (Simon, Findhorn, 3 January 1998)

> It's also a place here I've had the opportunity to practice service. Service. And service is not just about saying 'yes' and laying down and being a doormat, which I understood service as being through the church that I grew up in. I've come also to learn that service is taking care of myself as well as being willing to say 'yes' or 'no' as appropriate to whatever is presented to me in each moment of the day in the little things, in the day to day – just living and being and I happen to be doing it here, but I could be – it doesn't matter, it's like that community could be anywhere.
>
> (Terry, Findhorn, 3 January 1998)

Service then seems to be tied to community (sometimes expressed as place). This is an ancient conception of work that I should like now to further explore, as it is not unproblematic.

A notion of service can be found in many secular utopias of the Good Life. In *The Social Contract*, first published in 1762, Rousseau's ideal citizens submit themselves to the polis (Rousseau 1988). Their own particular and partial wills are submitted to the General Will, which is infallible and always serves the interests of the community. Likewise are Plato's Guardians, who occupy an ambiguous space that combines vanguard with submissive. Plato's ideal polity, as outlined in *The Republic* is at once elitist and egalitarian. The elite are the Guardians who protect and serve the state and the larger community. These people are those who are best equipped to fulfil the task. Their selection is somewhat opaque but Plato talks of selective breeding, of their education and also of the myth of 'The Forms' that should be told to the wider community in order to preserve stability.

Citizens, we shall say to them in our tale, you are brothers, yet God has formed you differently. Some of you have the power to command, and in the composition of these he has mingled gold, wherefore also they have the greatest honour; others he has made of silver, to be auxiliaries; others again who are to be husbandsmen and craftsmen he has composed of brass and iron and the species will generally be preserved in the children. But as all are of the same original stock, a golden parent will sometimes have a silver son, or a silver parent a golden son.

(Plato *Republic*, Bk. III)

The wider community – in the form of the State – is paramount. The happiness of the Guardians is not at issue:

our Guardians may very likely be the happiest of men, but our aim in founding the State was not the disproportionate happiness of any one class, but the greatest happiness of the whole. We mean our Guardians to be the true saviour and not destroyers of the State ... And therefore we must consider whether in appointing our Guardians we would look to their greatest happiness individually, or whether this principle of happiness does not rather reside in the State as a whole. But if the latter be the truth, then the Guardians and Auxiliaries, and all others equally with them, must be compelled or induced to do their own work in the best way.

(*ibid.*, Bk. IV)

The Guardians are required to serve the State; this is part of Plato's notion of a just society. The goal of this utopia is unity. The just society, for Plato, involves each person fulfilling the task to which their nature is best suited – and, consequently, a subjection of the self through service. I do not want to overstate the parallels between this view and that expressed at Findhorn and Erraid. The Findhorn Foundation is, however, referred to in terms such as a 'leading light' and a 'beacon that shines across the world' (Riddell 1996). There could be said to be an element of the vanguard in such vocabulary. There are further similarities with the Platonic conception of service. What irks in all of these accounts is the assumption that the good and virtuous citizen has access to a higher form of knowledge than do their fellow men. Such piety conceals a sublime arrogance that is present in most elitist world-views. Further, and perhaps more substantially, is a latent conception of power and authority. In whose name do the vanguard serve? Could service be a euphemism for leadership?

Possessions

It may be possible to think this through further by taking a more careful look at approaches to property more generally. I propose to do this in the first instance by taking a few steps back into the works of Rousseau and Plato.

Most people at Findhorn eschew personal materialism. Rousseau's citizens and Plato's Guardians do not have personal wealth. Another shared feature is the attitude to property *per se*. Rousseau's citizens give to the State themselves and their possessions:

> Every member of the community gives himself to it at the moment it is brought into being just as he is – he himself, with all his resources, including all his goods. (Rousseau, *Social Contract*, Bk. I, ch. 9)

Plato's Guardians have minimal personal possessions and no accumulated wealth. This is articulated in Plato's summary of the Guardian's life:

> In the first place, none of them should have any property of his own beyond what is absolutely necessary; neither should they have a private house or store closed against anyone who has a mind to enter; their possessions should be only such as are required by trained warriors, who are men of temperance and courage; they should agree to receive from the citizens a fixed rate of pay, enough to meet the expenses of the year and no more; they will go to the mess and live together like soldiers ... And they alone of all the citizens may not handle silver or gold, or be under the same roof with them, or drink from them. And this will be their salvation, and they will be the saviours of the State. (*Republic* Bk. III)

This austerity is not for its own sake, but rather goods are possessed according to need, as is judged appropriate to service. No surplus is permitted here. Greed is thus militated against. A commitment to material poverty and to work in service of the (internal) community and (external) society are often features of religious and spiritual communities (Knowles 1963). It is then unsurprising to find them at Findhorn Foundation communities. I should, however, like to briefly pursue this. In these accounts, a lack of personal possession is frequently equated with virtue and linked to social critique.

> Also, for me, there's such a space and opportunity here to let go of the trappings of modern society and to get back to what's simple and important.
> (Peter, Erraid, 28 August 1997)

> I look around, you know. The room I've got here and for those of you on tape, I've got a TV and I've got a desk and I've got a comfortable bed and I've got a guitar to play and I've got a music system and I've got CDs and so forth. However, this is it, you know. I have some stuff in boxes in Australia, but very little. I have no other home. What I've got here though is what sustains the things I have to give. Like I love music, playing the guitar, singing with people. I've got music sheets; I've got music to listen to which inspires me. I've got a TV and I use that very consciously ... Compared to my life – what I have owned, I've owned a house and owned two cars and

had the job and all that sort of stuff and I don't regret any of it, but I have no wish to go back to it, in fact it would, say, feel uncomfortable and I just don't want it.

(Terry, Findhorn, 3 January 1998)

Many Foundation members are former 'professionals' who have sold homes in order to finance their path through the hurdles of membership. Often too these people have been educated to University level. Some level of material 'sacrifice' has been made by all of the individuals to whom I spoke in these communities.

It could be the case that these accounts are expressions of self-delusion. The financial exchange on Erraid was, after all, just that: payment in return for accommodation and the privilege of living for a time in community. The financial-attunement ceremony could be cynically described as window dressing – or emotional blackmail. Working for free could be self-exploitation. Simple living could be articulated as an expression of pious self-congratulation. Again though I should like to suggest that the interpretation is less important than the fact that these accounts represents justifications and explanations of an alternative economy in which money and labour are conceived of in a way that is somehow different to mainstream society. These ideas are not new, as is evidenced by the brief excursion into the work of Plato and Rousseau. They are, however, utopian transgressions of the ways in which these relations are currently structured and contained.

Value

Looking at life in intentional communities permits us to imagine more fully the utopias of property that are articulated in the utopian canon. There is, in the long history of utopian writing, a tradition of critique regarding private property. This, too, is contained in ecological intentional communities. Thomas More's *Utopia* presents an inverted conception of wealth and value. Utopian writing, it should be remembered, always engages critically with contemporaneous debate (Sargisson 1996). Utopias are frequently critical of their own present society, politics and culture. Early in Book I of *Utopia*, the protagonist Hythloday is deeply critical of the Tudor system of social control and justice, and in particular of law and punishment in the case of crime against property. Other contemporaneous debates with which this book engages include the relation between crown and church, the role and nature of the State, the relation between the people and the monarch. The book was written during a changing period of economic infrastructure, and that too is explored. Less materially, *Utopia* explores intellectual debates within humanist thought namely the relation between morality and expediency.

The commentary in Book I on property sets the scene for entry into many of these debates. Hythloday is considering the problem of theft. The context of these comments is one in which the enclosure of common land was having a profoundly alienating effect upon the income and stability of many livelihoods. Idle mercenaries added to the problem, as did rising food prices. Theft had become a social problem of some magnitude, and the penalty for theft was death. Hythloday says of this:

> this manner of punishing thieves goes beyond justice and is not for the public good. It is too harsh a penalty for theft and yet is not a sufficient deterrent ... You ordain grievous and terrible punishments for a thief when it would have been much better to provide some means of getting a living, that no one should be under this terrible necessity of stealing and then of dying for it.
>
> (More 1965: Bk.I, 61)

He comments upon the social causes of widespread theft: the nobility and their retinues (the former he finds idle and the latter useless), retainers (maintained in case of war) and sheep – whence comes that memorable piece of satire:

> Your sheep ... which are usually so tame and so cheaply fed, begin now, according to report, to be so greedy and wild that they devour human beings themselves and devastate and depopulate fields, houses, and towns.
>
> (*ibid.*: 66–7)

The misappropriation of common land and its enclosure was a root cause of this and Hythloday describes fully the process of enclosure of land, expulsion of tenants and consequent social deprivation. He is clear that greed and a new concept of efficiency motivate this:

> Consequently, in order that one insatiable glutton and accursed plague of his native land may join field to field and surround many thousand acres with one fence, tenants are evicted.
>
> (*ibid.*: 67)

Little wonder then, he concludes, that the dispossessed should risk the penalties for theft. Their skills were inappropriate to the new farming techniques, there was a glut of available cheap labour, accommodation was scarce and inflation had made food unaffordable. It is clear from all of this that Hythloday is offering a radical and, considering the despotic nature of the monarch, dangerous set of criticisms of his (More's) time. Lest we be unconvinced as to the radicalism of his position, he goes on to fully spell out its implications. He proposes that the 'ruinous plagues' which are brothels and alehouses be forbidden (*ibid.*: 69). These are places in which people are encouraged to lose themselves in oblivion in the false hope of forgetting their troubles. He proposes that the law be changed such that those who are currently destroying the rural economy and infrastructure be forced to restore it. The rich should not, he says, have the unrestricted right to purchase. This speaks directly to concepts of ownership in which a thing owned is assumed to be at the full disposal of the owner. This account of ownership is dominant in current legal discourse and involves the right to have, possess and dispose of a thing (Waldron 1988). Further, says Hythloday, the agricultural revolution should be reversed in order that honest men can once again find employment, dignity and sustenance.

> Assuredly, unless you remedy these evils, it is useless for you to boast of the justice you execute in the punishment of theft. Such justice is more showy than really just or beneficial.
>
> (More 1965: 71)

By way of an aside, it is worth noting the style in which this is all couched. More employs rhetoric, a common device in sixteenth-century humanism. Fictional utopias, as a genre, allow the author a certain amount of freedom that might not fit so easily in a more conventional form of critique. More's book is subtle and complex. More invented the word, but not the genre of utopia: the good place (*eutopos*) which is no place (*outopos*). He uses form as well as content to engage in political critique. The above-sketched comment upon property is illustrative of this. Also though he uses style to enact critique, his rhetoric is focused in this case at those who would insist that the moral and the expedient are distinct.

> If the moral and the expedient are ultimately identical [as Stoics believed], then it is theoretically possible to design a commonwealth that would always act morally. But if the moral and the expedient cannot be fully reconciled [as Italian humanists such as Macchiavelli were suggesting], then this ideal could never be achieved, even in theory.
>
> (Morton 1952: 63)

This all points towards a reading of *Utopia* as a critical engagement in debate, rather than an attempt at a blueprint for future society. This has been well covered and I have suggested elsewhere that this is the most interesting way of thinking about utopias in general (Sargisson 1996). Further, there seems from this to be evidence of my suggestion that utopias permit us to think differently about political problems. By creating an imaginary world to explore, fictional utopias offer a space in which the commonplace problems of a given society can be estranged and re-viewed. This permits what I have been calling a paradigm shift in consciousness. With regards to More, the shift is one that moves thinking away from one of crime and punishment to include the wider social context which is thought to be responsible for the crime in the first place. Misuse of economic freedom and power combine, according to Hythloday, with human greed and indolence to generate a situation which is in social terms one of deprivation on the one hand and wealth on the other. Laws that are morally corrupt reinforce this.

The outcome not only involves physical poverty and crime but also a deprivation of esteem, as a whole class of worker's labour and skill is rendered worthless.

What's wrong with property?

I propose now to take this discussion one step further into the texts to think briefly about property in general. What, in the eyes of the historical utopias, is actually wrong with property? We see from Plato that those who hold political power ought not to have material wealth. Rousseau's citizens surrender themselves and their goods to the social contract. More is critical of the use of property by the nobility of the sixteenth century. This all looks quite diffuse and could be accounted for by various routes. We could, for instance, take a Hobbesian or Christian view of human nature as essentially flawed and self-serving. Property would then seem to serve our natural urge to dominate and flourish as individual maximisers of happiness (Hobbes 1968). However, I should like to explore the possibility that the utopian canon identifies property as a wrong in itself. If this is the case, then the alternative types of ownership outlined above might be of considerable theoretical significance. That they are of practical significance is, I think, clear. They are in this sense real-life examples of how to legally own things differently. I am concerned here to address the more difficult question of their status in theoretical terms. Can living differently help us to think differently about big and complex problems such as those involved in the ownership of property? This speaks to housing policy as well as to conceptual areas of equality, social justice and human nature.

> But should they [the Guardians] acquire homes or lands or moneys of their own, they will become housekeepers and husbandsmen instead of guardians, enemies and tyrants instead of allies of the other citizens; thing and being hated, plotting and being plotted against, they will pass their whole life in much greater terror of internal than external enemies, and the hour of ruin, both to themselves and to the rest of the Sate, will be at hand.
>
> (*Republic*, Bk. III)

Personal property then is, for Plato's Guardians, a distraction from their vocation. It encourages parochialism. It is an impediment to duty. Property ties man to the mundane and banal, it binds him to the commonplace and to be free from possessions in the way suggested permits transcendence of all of this and focus on higher matters. Similarly, Plato also implies here that personal possessions evoke rivalry and other 'lower' human emotions and motives. Again, to be free of property is to be above such concerns. These statements address human nature. His final statement: that Guardians who have no personal wealth are free from the fear of internal challenge is more pragmatic. The citizenry will not, he suggests, seek to usurp their Guardians if the leaders are in a state of material poverty. Of course, this denies the seeking of power for its own sake as human motivation, but is offered nonetheless in the spirit of *real Politik*: taking what is and acting with that.

More is similarly pragmatic:

> This wise sage [Plato] to be sure, easily foresaw that the one and only road to the general welfare lies in the maintenance of equality in all respects. I have my doubts that the latter could ever be preserved where the individual's possessions are his private property. When every man aims at absolute ownership of all the property he can get, be there never so great abundance of good, it is all shared by a handful who leave the rest in poverty. It happens generally that the one class pre-eminently deserves the lot of the other, for the rich are greedy, unscrupulous, and useless, while the poor are well-behaved, simple, and by their daily industry more beneficial to the commonwealth than to themselves. I am fully persuaded that no just and even distribution of goods can be made unless private property is utterly abolished. While it lasts, there will always remain a heavy and inescapable burden of poverty and misfortunes for by far the greatest and by far the best part of mankind.
>
> (More 1965: Bk. I, 105)

This argument against private property is couched in the vocabulary of social justice and exploitation, without reference to a universal human nature. Class bias makes this self-perpetuating, and it is clear that Hythloday feels this to be unjust on grounds of merit and desert. The fictional More, as presented in the book, disagrees with this, arguing that a decent standard of living requires the incentive of private personal gain. People will not work hard if they have nothing material to personally gain. This latter view recurs throughout debates on property and will be referred to below in the discussion of Basic Income Schemes.

The first thing that we are told about the state of Utopia is that there is no private property and that the people are industrious. Instead of sloth and shortage as foreseen by the fictional character of More, we find a land of equity and harmony. Homes are allocated by lot and changed every 10 years. Common ownership of homes occurs in many utopias (unsurprisingly, e.g., in those of the utopian socialists, and also in many contemporary feminist utopias). The Utopians have an inverted system of value when it comes to vernacular measures of wealth: gold and silver are denigrated and are worn by slaves. The story of the visiting dignitaries aptly illustrates both the power and the limitations of a worldview that is based on such an inversion. Hythloday tells the story of a group of diplomats from the country of Anemolius (often translated as Flatulentia). These visitors are described as 'more proud than wise' and 'determined to represent the gods themselves by their splendid adornment to dazzle the eyes of the poor Utopians.' (*ibid.*: 155). This they attempt by wearing bejewelled cloth of spun gold and much jewellery.

Hythloday tells the story with humour, describing how the children laugh at the dignitaries and how those more heavily adorned are assumed to be jesters or slaves. The gold chains around the necks of the ambassadors are criticised for being too thin and easily broken: what is the point of a chain that does not effectively bind? This shows something of the fun of *Utopia* as More playfully mocks the rationale of display. Satire is often a vehicle of critique in the utopian genre. Such descriptions make us smile and represent a partial transgression. They create a space in which challenges to the existing order can be played with, in which we can, perhaps, begin to imagine what a world without a conception of personal wealth might look like. This allows us also to challenge the validation of accepted sets of values (regarding, in this case, the concept of value itself).

> The Utopians wonder that any mortal takes pleasure in the uncertain sparkle of a tiny jewel when he can look at a star or even the sun itself. ... They wonder too that gold, which by its very nature is so useless, is now everywhere in the world valued so highly that man himself, through whose agency and for whose use it got this value, is priced much cheaper than gold itself.
>
> (*ibid.*: II, 57)

With these comments, More steps beyond the inversion of wealth and status that he creates in the story of the Anemdians, towards a critique of the construction of value itself. Utility and value are linked in this statement which is informed by egalitarianism and an assertion of inherent human worth. *Utopia* mocks the valuing of things that lack utility.

Property, in these utopias, encourages selfishness and lower emotions and behaviour. As such it is the focus of sustained criticism. It institutionalises unjust inequality and further serves the interests of a few individuals, rather than the State. This is not necessarily due to human nature but rather property provides an infrastructure in which the worst of man can flourish. It permits exploitation. It devalues human endeavour and denies the dignity of labour. As such we might say that it is dehumanising.

Property and work in intentional communities

In most intentional communities, paid work occurs outside of the home. However, people often work in part-time occupations. Material needs are less because consumer durables are shared and so, pragmatically, there is less need to earn the money to buy such items as washing machines and televisions. Mostly though it seems to be due to a different set of motivating priorities. Several people mentioned a lack of time as the reason why they work part-time. Guff, talking of a part time-job in a hostel for the homeless, explains that the job suits his particular needs:

I can come and go as I like, more or less, as long as I do 20 hours a week. It fits in with having my daughter ... [I used to do more] but I just didn't have much time. I was finding myself really pushed for time so I decided to drop the organic veg, being as it took up so much time. I was pretty sure it would continue without me so I thought this was the easiest thing to drop. That would give me an extra day and a half.

(Guff, Blackcurrant, 2 August 1997)

He says of the organic vegetable scheme:

Well I was one of the people who started it off at Blackcurrant and I've just stopped doing it last week. So that was going for years, most of the time for nothing. Just in the past year at most, we were paying ourselves 10–15 quid a week.

(Guff, Blackcurrant, 2 August 1997)

The scheme involves the purchase of organic fruit and vegetables and distribution at a minimal profit amongst 'customers' in the Northampton area. Originally, I was told, a bicycle (and trailer) were used for deliveries but recently the co-op has bought a van. This scheme never aimed at profit. It involves a large amount of time and labour: driving to the wholesalers, taking orders, sorting the produce, distribution. It benefits the co-op because it gives them access to produce that they could not otherwise afford, but it does not directly benefit individuals in any wage/labour exchange. I asked Guff why he started the scheme and gave it a day and a half of his time for so many years. He proceeded to tell me about organic farming and the use of fertilisers in non-organic crop production, finally summarising: 'Just because I believe in organic so much I suppose' (Guff, Blackcurrant, 2 August 1997). It seems fair to surmise that this labour was undertaken as a form of 'occupation' as opposed to 'employment'. The people at Blackcurrant expressed pride in their 'box scheme' and it gave them something less tangible than an income.

Detaching work from pay seems to have a number of effects. These concern the way in which we think about value in general, and self-worth in particular, and also to have structural implications.

(1) Value

Marx's theory of labour and value speaks directly to this. Marx outlines the way in which waged labour leads to exploitation by the owners of the means of production (property). Crudely put, workers have no access to the means of production and are compelled by this fact to sell their labour. Capitalists own the means of production and the end-product of the labour (which may be a combination of labour, raw materials and the process of production).

Labour produces not only commodities: it produces itself and the worker as a *commodity* – and does so in the proportion in which it produces commodities generally.

(Marx 1961: 69 cited in Caute 1967: 58)

This generates surplus value: the product is worth more than it has cost to produce and the workers are not paid this surplus. The owners of the factory or other means by which production was made possible appropriate the surplus. Labour is thus exploited:

> The product of labour is labour which has been congealed in an object, which has become material: it is the *objectification* of labour. Labour's realisation is its objectification. In conditions dealt with by political economy this realisa-tion of labour appears as a *loss of reality* for the workers; objectification is *loss of object* and *object-bondage*; appropriation as *estrangement*, as alienation.

(*ibid.*: 69)

Marx thus gives an account of how value equates with exploitation in a capitalist system. The utopias thus far consulted do not offer such systematic critique. They do, however, facilitate further exploratory consideration of this problematic concept and are, as such, useful and under-utilised vehicles for contemplation. Marx sees work *per se* as an essentially liberating phenom-enon. Mankind can achieve its fullest expression through praxis.

Work that is not for money exchange may represent a transgression of this exploitative relation. Conversely, as mentioned above, it may be the case that such endeavours are self-deluding. Malcolm at PIC is firmly of this view. Malcolm used to live at The Findhorn Foundation. Voluntary work, he maintains, is simply naive: labour should always be paid for. Voluntary work is self-exploitation. This is a challenging view.

Voluntary work is, it seems, used effectively and in a non-exploitative way by many intentional communities. Big projects sometimes necessitate a large input of labour. Examples might involve the upkeep or improvement of the land or buildings. When I visited Talamh, for instance, they had just erected a large poly-tunnel in the garden through a 'volunteer weekend' and Ian, whilst showing me around the 50 acres, explained how a newly established patch of mixed woodland had been accomplished over several weekends with the work of unpaid helpers. This would seem to be an effective way of utilising labour. Talamh's volunteer scheme is well organised and leaflets outline when help is needed and for what project. Most communities also welcome WWOOFERS – Willing Workers on Organic Farms – who receive food and shelter in return for work. I met several European students who were travelling the UK through this scheme, spending varying amounts of time at different communities, according to preference. However, this differs in degree and kind from the practices at Findhorn Foundation communities.

The passage below is a typical description of work from a member of the Findhorn Foundation:

I suppose one of the good aspects of the place is that because it's not, well, like as a student you pay to be here and then as a member you get enough to run a car basically. It means that you've got to be clear, you've got to be reasonably clear if you stay here longer, why – you know – why you're doing it because it's clearly not for the money and I think ... I've had the privilege of doing things because I wanted to do them and not because of thinking 'I need the money' which is a very freeing experience ...

I think that one of the most powerful lessons that this place teaches is about finding what you love doing or finding the meaning in whatever it is you're doing and learning to love whatever you're doing, I'm not sure that I'm so well advanced on that myself ...

(Patrick, Findhorn, 3 January 1998)

Here Patrick tells of the advantages of the Findhorn system, as he sees them. The system does, however, have its critics even within the Foundation. Full 'staff' members of the Foundation exist in a state of relative poverty and this does prevent many people from taking the step to membership. Questions are currently being asked about this in internal debates and some argue the case for a more generous allowance and a shorter working week. This, it is argued, would still relieve people of the perceived pressure to work for money, but would also relieve them of their continual strain of worrying about their own personal finances. The link between wage and work could be broken without the need for poverty.

(2) Self-worth

Marx identifies the profoundest alienation as one consequence of waged labour in a capitalist economic system. The worker is alienated materially from the surplus value of his labour – as outlined above. S/he is further alienated from the product of this labour, as 'efficient' production-line systems de-skill the labour force and diminish the sense of both competence and ownership felt over the final product. This finds full expression in *Capital* (Vol. I):

The knowledge, the judgement, and the skill, which, though in ever so small a degree, are practised by the independent peasant or handicraftsman ... these faculties are now required only for the workshop as a whole. Intelligence in production expands only in one direction because it vanishes in many others. ... Some crippling of body and mind is inseparable from division of labour in society as a whole. Since, however, manufacture carries this social separation much further, and also, by its peculiar division, attacks the individual at the roots of his life, it is the first to afford the materials for, and to give starts to, industrial pathology.

(Marx 1961: 361–3)

Workers are also alienated from one another and, at a deeper level, from a sense of self-worth. Marxist feminists have revised this to include also procreative work in consideration of production and domestic labour as work. Unwaged domestic work, they argue, should be given economic status: the International Wages for Housework Campaign has been making this case for years. An allowance paid by the State, or a social wage, is one way in which Marxist and socialist feminists have attempted to engage with this. At root is a critique that takes that offered by Marx one step further: women in particular, it is argued (though we might want also to include here anyone who 'works' in the informal economy) are denied the sense of self-worth that comes with waged labour. Financial independence is intimately connected to liberal accounts of the autonomous individual, a point that was not lost on early suffragettes who argued for women's access into the public sphere of work and money.

An alternative way of approaching this might be to sever the link between money and work. The people who live in communities where this is common practice certainly seem to have a strong sense of self-worth and empowerment which arises directly from their work.

> There is such a long history of people having to prove their worth through their job. That's why it's so devastating when people don't have jobs. There is a need to establish an identity that's a worthwhile identity.
>
> (Elizabeth, Erraid, 27 July 1997)

There may also be opportunity within a culture of part-time work – or the non-waged economy of Erraid and Findhorn, to experiment with a variety of different forms of work. This too is described in terms of personal empowerment and self-worth:

> the work is such a grounding aspect of life here, it's like, because it's such difficult work, someone like me who comes from a publishing background – communication background – I work very much with the brain and communicating with people on a sort of mental level and emotional level and coming to a place where physical life is so fundamental, it's so refreshing to me because my brain is very much used and my intellect and communicating sense is very useful and within that I'm really using my body in a new way. I think that's really enlivening, really enriching, and because the work is basically pretty simple and unskilled, it means that anyone can have a go ...
>
> (Katie, Erraid, 29 July 1997)

It would, however, be misleading to suggest that severing the connection between wage and work on Erraid has the magical and automatic effect of solving problems of self-esteem. This is an apparent subtext of the statement below, which again comes from Katie:

Now people talk about work-aholism and I think a lot of people on Erraid who live here long term are really into work and some of them identify themselves very much with their work and there is that aspect of people being, you know, 'work, work' sort of attached to working hard and ... they can make a pressure on themselves to work hard and I see that happening and you know you have to be quite strong within yourself not to get caught up in 'Oh I'm not valuable unless I'm working hard enough'.

(Katie, Erraid, 29 July 1997)

(3) Time and structural implications

From what Guff says above it seems clear that a different way of thinking about time is occurring in his reasoning. The day consists not of what can be fitted around work, but *vice versa*. Is there room for paid work in my life, given all the other interests and commitments that I have? Asked what, if anything, is wrong with modern society, Peter began thus:

It's impossible to know where to start. Lots. Jobs to earn money – 'life' at the weekend. Something is lacking – so materialist. And in that empty space there seems to be so much fear – generated fear – nonsense in the media – which takes over because there's an emptiness.

(Peter, Erraid, 28 July 1997)

At People in Common, Shaun works part time at the co-operatively owned hardwood centre as well as working on computer-training sessions and youth projects. Paul, at the same community, works part time with the charity Jigsaw which is a training organisation, aimed at placing people with learning difficulties in paid employment. This charity aims to gain for so-called 'unemployable' people the respect and material good that come from paid work. Successful examples of their work are a young woman who has been taken on by The Body Shop, and those who work in the charity's own cafe and market stall.

Is the severance of work and pay then a transgressive and utopian act? Does it, in other words, facilitate the creation, experience or imagination of something new and different? Does it enact a critique and create a space in which paradigm shifts can be explored? To respond with an unqualified affirmative would be to overstate and oversimplify a complex, contradictory set of circumstances, but I do believe there to be interesting and creative things occurring here. The different systems (or anti-systems) in the different communities can in different ways inform and perhaps inspire. The value of work as an expression and manifestation of self-worth is apparent in all the communities that I visited, and in most cases the work undertaken is occupying and engaging, though not necessarily income-generating. In some cases, such as at Blackcurrant, the work is an expression of a political or ethical commitment. Likewise Findhorn. In others, work is an expression of a different set of personal priorities. On one level, albeit that of superficial resemblance, the system at Findhorn is not unlike basic income schemes as advocated by some green economic theory and which I shall discuss further below. First though, some more general comments on the relation between work and wages.

The focus of green critique is on attitudes to work and especially on the ways in which work is associated with pay:

> Such an association can lead us to believe that if a person is not in paid employment then they are not working. This, for greens, is simply untrue, and their re-negotiation of the meaning of work leads them to suggest ways of freeing it from what they see as restrictions founded on the modern (and archaic) sense that work is just paid employment.
>
> (Dobson 1995: 104)

Andrew Dobson outlines four components of the deep ecological critique of leisure-based utopia in which there is no work. This, he says, is a common scenario in which 'clean' technology labours for us and leisure is increased.

(1) greens raise questions of sustainability on a finite planet;
(2) automated production, it is believed, will cause unemployment;
(3) such a society would be greatly divided 'between the highly paid monitors of machinery and the stinted recipients of social-security payments pitched at a level designed to discourage indolence;
(4) leisure industry is detrimental to the Good Life because it encourages consumption and a lack of self-discipline (Dobson 1995: 104–6).

At the root of this is a belief that work is good for us. An old-style Protestant Work Ethic haunts this view of the world, which asserts the value of work for self-mastery and autonomy as well as imbibing green values of sustainable development. The fear articulated here of the development of a new class-based society based on work clearly has socialist roots. Green political thought is indeed a curious hybrid. The view that work is good for us, for instance, has ancient roots that predate Christianity but which seriously inform that view. Jonathan Porritt, cited in Dobson, evokes St Thomas Aquinas when describing his own approach to work:

> There can be no joy of life without the joy of work, that just about sums it up for me.
>
> (Porritt 1984 in Dobson 1995: 105)

Work forms an important part of Plato's view of the ideal polity which he describes in terms of justice. The just state is like the just man: it is internally balanced and harmonious. This means that each person is occupied in the best way, which is suited to his or her individual nature. Reason, desire and

spirit, or passion are balanced within the man who is in a state of justice, and
he finds employment appropriate to his nature. Likewise, in the just state,
those best suited to a certain occupation find it:

> You remember the original principle which we were always laying down at
> the Foundation of the State, that one man should practice one thing only,
> the thing to which his nature was best adapted; – now justice is this
> principle, or a part of it.
>
> *(Republic*, Bk. IV)

There is an inherent conservatism here and an essentialism, neither of which I
have the space to fully explore. The point that I should like to note is that,
for Plato, work or occupation (in the literal sense) transcends paid labour
and forms a central ingredient of the Good Society. This is true also of other
utopian thinkers to whom I shall refer below. The essentialism of this view is
not of great importance to this current enquiry, and neither is the fact that
Plato's prescription is in many ways antithetical to the reality explored in contemporary intentional communities. Rather, I should like to stress again
that utopias – as literary or physical spaces – represent an opportunity for
thinking differently about something that we might otherwise take for
granted. In a money economy work is for wage. Utopian philosophy, such as
is engaged in *The Republic*, facilitates a thorough interrogation of this 'reality'
and attempts to imagine how things might be better and different. The
premise is that work is good for us and that it is integral to the human
condition: that men are most fully stretched and expressive of their natures
when engaged in fulfilling and appropriate work. This is more important to
Plato than is remuneration, as can be seen by his denial of personal wealth to
those at the 'top' of his social hierarchy. For Plato it is in the interest of both
the state and the individual that affairs be thus balanced. Stability and
harmony can, he suggests, be found through such internal unity and
coherence.

William Morris, in *News from Nowhere* (1993), makes the separation of work and
money explicit. The utopia visited by William Guest is a non-money economy,
of which more later. Guest wakes to find himself in another 'world' – he is
somewhere other than his home in which he fell asleep. Wondering, he accepts a
ride from a boatman he finds outside what was once his house (now the 'guest-
house'). His offer of payment is met with puzzlement:

> You see this ferrying and giving people casts about the water is my *business*,
> which I would do for anybody; so to take gifts in connection with it would
> look very queer.
>
> (Morris 1993: 7)

Ferrying, then, is this man's occupation. It is not a trade in economic terms of
exchange. In this utopia, work is flexible to allow people a mixture of indoor

and outdoor and mental and physical exercises. When the boatman leaves his post to act for a while as guide to Guest, a friend who is a weaver is given the opportunity to take on the ferry. The boatman plans to go and help with a harvest and also enjoys creative metalwork. Morris was, of course, engaged in the Arts and Craft Movement and this is one of the contemporary debates with which this utopia engages. This theme of varied occupation is more common in the history of utopian writing than is Plato's vision of one man, one job. Marx's higher form of communism has the well-known fisher/critic scenario (Marx 1844: 22). Charles Fourier's utopia phalansteries permit the communards to flit between tasks like butterflies:

> That the industrial sessions be varied about eight times a day, it being impossible to sustain enthusiasm longer than an hour and a half or two hours in the exercise of agricultural or manufacturing labour.
>
> (Fourier 1901: 64)

Work, in these (socialist) utopias is potentially satisfying and fulfilling, and the self-appointed task of the utopian is to construct the best and most appropriate system for the achievement of this potential. The background to this is a view of work as a good thing. Work is a virtuous activity. It is fulfilling (in a non-exploitative setting).

> 'The reward of labour is *life*. Is that not enough?'
> 'But the reward for especially good work?' quoth I
> 'Plenty of reward,' said he, 'the reward of creation. The wages which God gets, as people might have said in time agone.'
>
> (Morris 1993: 77)

Guest asks how this society arrived at this happy condition and is told the following:

> By the absence of artificial coercion, and the freedom for every man to do what he can do best, joined to the knowledge of what productions of labour we really want.
>
> (*ibid.*: 79)

This, incidentally, leads to the creation of products of high and beautiful quality such as Guest's tobacco pouch that he is given to replace his own rather shabby one (*ibid.*: 30–2). Work, this suggests, can be satisfying in and for itself – and this is to the benefit of the individual and society. The result is high-quality produce, satisfied craftsmen and a good society. The worker has the sense of ownership over the process of production that is identified in Marxian critiques as absent in capitalist society. This is tied to the non-ownership of the final product. The beautiful tobacco pouch is given to

Guest. It is described as a labour of love and is given freely away to someone who will enjoy it.

This brings again to mind the quote from Paul at PIC:

> It's non-possessive ownership.
>
> (Paul, PIC, 1 October 1998)

Mike, also at PIC, speaks here of how he felt at Lifespan, another intentional community, about the garden:

> Lifespan was the first garden that I could call my own in terms of, you know, not 'mine' possessive, but mine in terms of action. Lifespan was the first place I could walk out of the door and into a garden which I, you know, had a commitment to, yeah, that's better than 'mine': a garden that I had a personal commitment to. . . . My creative expression is myself as a gardener.
>
> (Mike, PIC, 20 Sptember 1997)

Despite a sense of commitment and ownership then, the relationship that Mike is trying to describe is not one of private possession. Nor is it merely one of contingency or utility. There is, in addition to the pragmatism of Mike's approach, also an articulation of another, different way of thinking about ownership and the fruits of one's labour. Mike talks here about his hopes for a gift economy with the wider community. The produce of the garden is the result of the unwaged labour and expertise of Mike and Paul:

> The moment we get people coming down here saying, you know, 'Ok if we take some raspberries?' 'Have you got any spare garlic?' or whatever, then they're sort of . . . it's like getting people from the outside to actually demand, you know, their share in our resources and obviously we'll get abused at some points . . . and at that point we'll have to deal with it. Learning how to deal with this kind of thing is one of the primary by-products of intentional communities.
>
> (Mike, PIC, 20 Sptember 1997)

Alternative economies?

Within the 'mainstream'

One practical consequence of breaking the connection between wages and work relates to the re-conception roles of the public and the private spheres, discussed in the previous chapter. If meaningful work is not just employment for wages outside of one's own home, then domestic labour and the informal economy become available for consideration as 'work'. One implication of this is a re-conceptualisation of economic measures such as Gross National Product. Green economist Victor Anderson suggests, as a way of measuring economic indicators, that both non-money transactions and the value of unpaid labour be included in what he calls an 'Adjusted National Product' (Anderson in Dobson 1995: 106). Whilst this is a radical innovation, it does not sever the connection altogether from money and a property-based economy. Rather it seeks a revaluation of unwaged (exploitative) labour in the informal economy in terms appropriate to the formal economics of money and work and value.

Feminist economic and social theorists have long since stressed the value of work done in the informal economy. Briefly, women's oppression in the home is connected, in many feminist critiques, to women's historical experiences of subordination in and exclusion from the workplace. Commentators point out that not only is it still commonplace that women take responsibility for a large proportion of housework and child-rearing, but also they are frequently engaged in other unpaid caring work in the wider community (Witz 1993).

From this empirical observation, feminist theorists take the debate in interesting directions. An example of one approach comes from Joan Tronto, who insists that care is a political concept. She mobilises care to enable a re-conceptualisation of 'the political'. For Tronto, care is

> a species activity that includes everything that we do to maintain, continue, and repair 'our world' so that we can live in it as well as possible.
>
> (Fischer and Tronto in Tronto 1996)

Care is, she says, excluded from politics because it is considered apolitical, or pre-political (Aristotle) – or, because it is thought to be above politics (Augustine). This latter view takes the suffering and charity of Christ to be a model for Christian charity. More materially, she suggests also that care is excluded from political debate because it occurs in the informal, unwaged, economy or in the low-status waged extensions of this: nursing, childcare, school teaching. Introducing care into the sphere of the political allows what she claims to be a

> richer, more genuine, and more pluralistic account of equality and democratic life. When we include care and those who care in the political arena, we recognise that citizens are not self-sufficient. ... Recognition of our mutual status of dependence and conditions of vulnerability provides a different basis for equality.
>
> (Tronto 1996: 149)

I mention Tronto's work in this area as an example of an attempt at a paradigm shift in the way that we think about work. Tronto's work operates on a theoretical level. More materially, work, as a phenomenological activity, is the focus of the thought of feminists from all aspect of the ideological spectrum. Betty Freidan (1981) exemplifies a liberal view. She calls for a basic re-structuring of work patterns (thus allowing men and women to engage in homecare and the care of children). Elsewhere in feminist thought, the liberal ideal of the autonomous and rational actor is challenged and expanded by reference to the informal economy. Alison Jagger, for instance, introduces nurturence, co-operation and care into her socialist critique as characteristics that she argues are essential to a good and functioning society (Jagger 1983). I have already mentioned the work of Marxist feminists, who introduce reproduction into discussions of production labour and procreation into a critique of creative work (Buckley 1989). The point of relevance to this enquiry is that, ideological perspective aside, any attempt at privileging the informal economy has far-reaching consequences at a conceptual level. This further relates to the discussion in Chapter 3 of the public and private spheres.

Other suggestions for change within the existing economic infrastructure include basic income schemes. These are seen by greens as a way of reconciling the formal and informal economies. Basic income schemes are not, of course, the sole property of green political thought. However, I shall begin my discussion in this terrain because greens view work *per se* to be of inherent value and attempt a paradigm shift in our thinking about work and money. Paul Ekins writes of the green desire for a 're-conceptualisation of the nature and value of work' (Ekins 1986: 97). He considers this to be a central pillar of green social and economic theory. Clearly a change in practices goes part way toward this. What is needed though, for a sustainable and grounded shift, is an account of why we need to work differently. This is where the concept of transgressive utopianism is of value as it facilitates the kind of conceptual shift required to accompany changes in daily practice.

Known variously as Minimum Income Schemes (MIS) or Guaranteed Basic Income Schemes (GBIS), proposals for the provision of a basic income are neither new nor the unique property of any one ideology. Charles Fourier provides for a basic income in his early utopian socialism.

> It is necessary, in order that it become attractive, that associative labour fulfils the following eight conditions:
>
> 1   That every labourer be a partner, remunerated by dividends and not by wages.
> 2   That every one, man, woman, or child, be remunerated in proportion to the three faculties: *capital, labour, and talent.*
> 3   That the industrial sessions be varied about 8 times a day . . .
> 4   That they be carried on by bands of friends united spontaneously and stimulated by active rivalries.
> 5   That the workshops and husbandry offer the labourer the allurements of elegance and cleanliness.
> 6   That the division of labour be carried out to the last degree, so that each sex and age may devote itself to duties that are suited to it.
> 7   That in this distribution, each one – man, woman, or child – be in full

enjoyment of the right to labour or the right to engage in such branch of labour as they may please to select . . .

8   Finally, that, in this new order, people possess a guarantee of well-being of maximum sufficient for the present and the future and that this guarantee free from all uneasiness concerning themselves and their families.

(Fourier 1901: 164)

The most interesting contemporary vision of a just society based on guaranteed income comes from Philippe Van Parjis. This scheme is considered and thoughtful. It proposes a vision of a just society in which a capitalist economic system offers to all its members a basic income. Again, what makes this interesting is its attempt at a radical shift in approach to work and money within a given economic (property based) system of exchange. The income is to be generous and unconditional. Coincidentally, Van Parjis has a personal history that connects to intentional communities:

Work on this book started in the rainy spring of 1977, as I was settling down in a small green commune within hitching distance of Beilfeld University. What exactly is fundamentally wrong, I wanted to find out, with the capitalist societies we live in?

(Van Parjis 1995: vi)

One thing that marks out this approach is Van Parjis' transgression of the left/right polemic that often accompanies this terrain. He engages seriously with the neo-liberal defence of capitalism and is suspicious of the claim that either pure capitalism or pure socialism can best facilitate a free society. His premise is twofold:

One: Our capitalist societies are replete with unacceptable inequalities.
Two: Freedom is of paramount importance.

(*ibid.*: 1)

His aim is what he calls 'real libertarianism' or the titular 'real-freedom-for-all' (*ibid.*: 1). The capitalist or mixed economies of Western Europe can, he argues, afford and could implement a basic income scheme that would offer sustenance to all. Freedom, for Van Parjis, is as follows: 'It is the freedom to live as one might like to live' (*ibid.*: 30). Part of this is the libertarian freedom to purchase and consume with an interesting rider: namely, that this should be so irrespective of work. The larger aim of this is control over one's life:

The real freedom we need is not just the freedom to choose among the various bundles of goods one might wish to consume. It is the real freedom to choose among the various lives that one might like to lead.

(*ibid.*: 33)

Hence unconditionally. A really freeing income is, he says, the highest possible one. General advantages of basic income schemes are said to include the fact they remove structural disincentives for part time and voluntary work. This enables social groups like lone parents, who might not be able to work full time or to survive financially on part-time wages, to engage in what might be considered socially useful and personally satisfying work. It also encourages a more flexible approach to the working day, which is said by some to be more in tune with people's natural rhythms. This speaks to New Age practices such as those at Findhorn Foundation communities, where working hours are aimed at nurturing personal energy and work is aimed at self-realisation. However, whilst this is appropriate to Findhorn, it does not entirely apply to the other communities.

People in Common used to have an income pool, which is a different concept altogether but does have an egalitarian end in terms of outcome. No community that I visited had a working income pool, though there are some: examples are Crabapple and Glaneirw, neither of which was open to visitors at the time of this research. Most income-pooling communities are spiritual: convents and monasteries frequently operate on this basis. Pooling income requires a certain amount of trust and unity. The pool at PIC lasted for 20 years. Derek, a founding member of this community, explained to me why, in his view, it had worked for so long:

> I think the reason it worked was because we had this enormous project doing the place up and the only way to do it was to do that [pool incomes] and when it was finished people relaxed and thought 'Oh, I could do some other things with this earning power I have now. I'm not sure I want to do the same thing as everybody else anymore.' And so it became more and more difficult to hold it together but for a long time, when there was a central aim, that's what we did and I actually quite liked that, even though I was one of the higher earners at the time.
>
> (Derek, PIC, 1997)

Income pooling is not a micro basic income scheme. It is fundamentally different. These communities are small intimate spaces into which each member contracts deliberately. The pool is a conscious bond, focused apparently at a common purpose. It is, however, similar to a basic income scheme in its aims and origins: it is idealistic as well as pragmatic. It aims to create a working alternative to current property relations, within a larger context. The easy criticism of basic income schemes is that 'people aren't like that' and freeloading will drag the whole system down. At some communities that I visited there was clear disparity of labour and commitment to the community. But in each case the individuals showing a disinclination to commit time and energy have now (12 months later) left the community. It was more common to find that members took responsibility for a certain area of work that suited their circumstances and skills.

Patrick, at Findhorn, makes an interesting observation regarding responsibility and the ownership of process in work. For many years he focalised (managed) the kitchen at Cluny. Cluny is where most of the guests stay at the Findhorn Foundation, and caters for over a hundred people at most meals. There is a small skeleton staff of permanent members and long-term guests, which is supplemented by visitors who are assigned or attuned to work there. This means that meals are cooked by an ever-changing (sometimes daily) group of people. Managing this process must be difficult:

> I see someone who's making soup and I see that they're not really paying very much attention and that the soup's burning because they're off chatting … and one way is that I could turn the soup off or say 'Hey! The soup's burning, you'd better do something about it' or I can (can I?) at times it's like just trusting that the most appropriate thing is to just leave it and that's the only way they'll learn not to burn, to pay attention, is to let them burn the soup and to have that experience and see the consequences and to know what responsibility is.
>
> (Patrick, Findhorn, 3 January 1998)

Letting go is a key characteristic of what, in deconstructive theory, is called a feminine or Gift economy. This is a utopian conception of how social relations might be otherwise mediated and I should like to briefly explore this now. All of the innovations discussed thus far have taken capitalist property relations as they are and represent practical or theoretical attempts to re-negotiate things within the existing system. This utopian economy is a transgressive conception of how to exchange goods and self.

Without the 'mainstream'

Gift economics

Some of the most interesting recent work done in this area comes from Judith Still (1997). Still identifies the gift in opposition to what she calls 'the market' (*ibid*.: 2). Each of these is an economy and each has a driving paradigm and a motivating logic.

> The logic of the market is that everyone works for wages and that leisure (broadly encompassing indolence and the time in which to perform exploits) becomes a good to be purchased.
>
> (Still 1997: 2)

There are, she says, two influential sources of this logic: neo-classical economics and Marxism. Despite their differences, both of these traditions are antithetical to the notion of the gift economy (*ibid*.: 3). Market economics takes value as a fixable term, value is assumed to be quantifiable and commensurate. Value mediates exchange, and exchange is the driving force of a market economy. A gift economy is not driven by exchange. It is not concerned with efficiency but is preoccupied by ethics. It assumes abundance of supply and gives freely. This, she says, may be achieved by the expansion of supply, or by re-conceiving demand.

Two thinkers who contribute originally to this debate are Helene Cixous and Jacques Derrida. Cixous terms the economies as libidinal. The feminine is 'open' and transgresses the masculine, which is a closed economy. Derrida uses the vocabulary of the Proper and the Gift. My focus in the introductions below is on the useful ways in which Derrida enables us to negotiate the vocabulary of property.

Derrida

Derrida's 'poststructuralism' goes beyond conventional critical practice and beyond the way in which we are accustomed to conceptualise things. It resists structure and order and takes us to a new/no place that has some bearing on the understanding of utopianism that informs this book. This utopianism is open-ended and forbids closure, and I should like to suggest that Derrida's work does the same. His work operates by deconstruction, which is best described for current purposes as a process of reading. It stems from a tradition that sees a relation between language and thought as lacking innocence.

Speaking, writing and articulating our thought are, in this view, a series of actions within a political process in which power is constantly distributed and relations of power are constantly reaffirmed. Put simply: language orders thought. Language has its own economy and this economy is of the same nature as the wider social and economic exchange which Still calls 'the market'. Deconstruction is an attempt to disrupt the flow of construction and affirmation of order. It works always within – inside of – the text. Text here can be understood either in the narrow sense of a written text or/and in the wider and more encompassing sense of a cultural text. To try to work outside of the text would be utopian in a negative sense: it would be impossible – ridiculous. This is because the (cultural) text is thought to write us even as we speak. We are inscribed by the text: part of it, and largely, products of its economy.

This is not to say that people have no individuality, or that the *status quo* is inevitable. Resistance is possible and this is one function of deconstruction. Deconstruction is highly technical and I shall explain its mechanics again in the next chapter. Briefly, it attempts to work in between oppositional pairs of concepts, which are constructed with mutual reference, but which embody relations of exclusion and power. Property is an interesting concept with which to work in this way because it has no immediately apparent Other. Derrida constructs the (utopian) Gift as Other to Property. For present purposes, the Proper and the Gift might be said to be utopian constructions. It is on the Proper that I shall now focus.

The Proper

The Proper is, according to Derrida, driven by the desire to appropriate: to take for oneself (power, money and status).

Derrida's sources are eclectic. His work on property draws in part upon Freudian and Lacanian psychoanalyses as well as on the structuralist thought of Ferdinand de Saussure. In thinking about what he calls the Drive of the Proper, (a motivating psychoanalytic drive), Derrida plays with the word 'proper', from which the concepts of 'property' and 'appropriation' derive. All meanings invoked by these terms conflate in his reading of the Proper. In the English language, property has an interesting collection of associations:

Proper:

1. Own; 2. Belonging, relating to, exclusivity to; 3. Name used to designate an individual person, animal, etc; 4. Accurate, correct; 5. Real, genuine; 6. Thorough, complete; 7. Handsome; 8. Fit, suitable, right; 9. In conformity with standards of society; 10. In the natural state.

Property:

1. Owning, being owned, thing owned, possessions; 2. Article of costume, furniture, used on stage; 3. Attribute, quality.

Appropriate:

1. Take possession of, take to oneself, devote to special purposes; 2. Belonging, peculiar, suitable, proper, correct.

The Drive of the Proper, says Derrida, impels us towards appropriation: the appropriate and correct way to be.

For Derrida this complex term informs social exchange, which is mediated by language. Language is connected to possession beyond the grammatical sense. He emerges from his work on this with a view of naming – describing articulating and giving sense to a thing – as an act in which power is appropriated.

The value of this contribution lies in the different perspective that it brings to discussions of property. Further, it permits connection of the somewhat disparate discussions above in a more or less coherent narrative. If property relations are driven by the desire to appropriate for oneself the power (economic, social, sexual) of others, then property comes to occupy a central role in political thought. I began this chapter with an assertion that property is at once marginal and central to political theory and I should like to re-stress this. Consideration of property relations speaks to all other social and political relations. If this is so, then the ways in which we own our home, the ways in which we think about ownership: how many possessions we have, how and why we work. All of these things go beyond their own parameters to connect to wider debates about how to 'be'. Negotiation of these questions of apparent property may, in other words, help us to address wider questions of human relationships. This is the focus of the next chapter.

The Gift

There are parallels between the ways in which deconstruction is argued to operate and the claims that I make for utopian thought. Both are part of that which they critique. Yet both are estranged in some way: utopias offer visions of places that are (spatially and/or temporally) far away, deconstruction creates moments in which it may be possible to think differently about the world (Sargisson 1996: 105). Both are simultaneously critical and creative. I have argued above that intentional communities operate in a physical sense in ways similar to literary and theoretical utopias. The Gift is a utopian concept: a theoretical construct which, I suggest, represents a space for exploration and development of alternative ways of being. What makes the Gift so interesting is that it is not possible in an economy driven by the Drive of the Proper. It is impossible: materially and conceptually. We can see glimmers of it in some moments of deconstruction, but cannot fully articulate it as a concept. Not, at least, without a paradigm shift in the way that we think. Not without constant awareness of the words that we (have to) use and their attendant baggage: their properties.

An example of a gift in a Property economy can be found in the Old Testament:

> In the beginning God created the heaven and the earth.
> And the earth was without form, and void; and darkness was upon the face of the deep.
> And the Spirit of God moved upon the face of the waters.
> And God said, Let there be light: and there was light.
>
> (Genesis I)

In the beginning was the Word, and the Word was God. As the root of all names and of all things, God owns the power of naming and of creation. It is his possession: in his gift.

> In giving his name, a name of his choice, in giving all names, the father [God] would be at the origin of language, and that power would belong by right to God the father.
>
> (Derrida 1985: 246)

This is not though a 'true' gift. It is not free: there is a return. The return is that of omnipotence. The fantasy then of the Gift is non-reciprocity. This has certain resonance with New Age rhetoric regarding love, to which I shall return in Chapter 5. Briefly though, there is in this worldview a commitment to 'unconditional love': love without expectation or contractual return.

To suggest that Britain's intentional communities inhabit a post-structuralist Gift economy would be bizarre. It is, however, possible to give a post-structuralist account of their internal economies, which do indeed have an Other (different and estranged) dynamic. As such, the communities represent a space in which transgressive and utopian thought can be further explored. Because they have different practices and offer accounts for these, which deviate from the standard discourse of ownership, the communities do provide material for this kind of exercise. This, I think, is methodologically interesting. Pragmatically, this exercise permits further imagining of how the Good Life might be conceptualised and actualised and it is to this that I shall turn in Chapter 5 on Self/Other Relations.

Conclusion

Discussion in this chapter has been wide ranging and has touched on a number of areas that I should like now to briefly re-visit. The communal method of ownership (namely co-operative ownership) permits people to own a part of what is in most cases a high-quality living space. This is possible without access to or ownership of large amounts of personal wealth. What is owned is part of a beautiful home – and a £1 share in the Co-op. This raises a number of interesting questions connected to the following areas:

- value;
- conceptualising ownership and property;
- relationship to place.

Work in communities sometimes appears to sever the connection of labour to property, which dominates the money economy. People's accounts of this speak to some interesting theoretical debates:

- self-worth;
- identity;
- value;
- the nature of exploitation.

I have gestured towards two very different approaches to this that come from the worlds of political philosophy: the basic income scheme and the utopia of a gift economy.

The utopian bodies of thought to which I have referred enable further exploration of these areas. Utopias, I have argued throughout, are an invaluable resource for political thought. Not only do they offer critique, but they also add to this imagination and play and creativity. In addition, they are spaces (physical, fictional, imaginary and real) in which we can think about things differently. As self-contained discrete spaces they offer to the actor or thinker a certain security. As easily identifiable spaces, they can act as points of inspiration. Visitors from the mainstream can enter them and engage in utopian dialogue, returning marked by the encounter. In this way, to use post-structuralist vocabulary, we can, perhaps, begin to re-inscribe alternative relations (of property, in this instance) onto the culture that we inhabit.

5   Self/Other relations

Many people – many nations – can find themselves holding, more or less wittingly, that 'every stranger is an enemy'. For the most part this conviction lies deep down like some latent infection; it betrays itself only in random, disconnected acts, and does not lie at the base of a system of reason. But when this does come about, when the unspoken dogma becomes the major premise in a syllogism, then, at the end of the chain, there is the Lager.[1] Here is the product of a conception of the world carried rigorously to its logical conclusion; so long as the conception subsists, the conclusion remains there to threaten us. The story of the death camps should be understood by everyone as a sinister alarm-signal.

(Primo Levi, writing of Auschwitz. Levi 1979: 15)

Introduction

Analysis of the Self/Other relation is central to green political thought. It speaks to the ways in which we think about ourselves in relation to the world: as individuals who are in relationship with other individuals and in broader terms as members of various groups. Identity lies close to the heart of this debate. My concern is partly with the actual character of Self/Other relations as empirically observable. Also, and perhaps more importantly, this chapter is concerned to examine the ways in which accounts of these relationships are constructed and interpreted. I am, in other words, interested in both the relations themselves and in the conceptualisation of these relations.

My claim that Self/Other relations are central to green political thought may appear perverse. More sustainable, surely, to claim that our attitude to animals and the environment lie beneath our ecological or other behaviour? Should not the relationship of humanity to nature be the focus of research? Greens are known for their affection for the 'roots' of a problem. Their approach is holistic. Part of holistic consciousness involves an awareness of the entirety of apparently local issues. Acid rain in Wales, for instance, is not just regarded as a local problem of pollution – it is a consequence of industrial activity in other locations; of patterns

---

[1] German extermination camp of World War II.

of consumption; of lifestyles and wants. To really 'solve' the problem of acid rain, many greens would say, requires more than clean industry. It requires, amongst other things, a radical shift in consciousness. David Pepper, in *The Roots of Modern Environmentalism*, argues that knowing the facts of environmental degradation is but one step towards being a part of what he calls 'environmental politics':

> It will be no good bombarding us with 'facts' which we are anyway predisposed to dismiss. A wiser strategy would be to shake the foundations of our beliefs by undermining the assumptions on which they are based.
>
> (Pepper 1989: 2)

I suggest that relations of Self to Other provide the grounding for the ways in which we think about our environment. Notwithstanding this, green concerns regarding what I call Self/Other relations are frequently articulated through explorations of humanity's relationship with the 'natural' world:

> What we do about ecology depends on our *ideas* of the man–nature relationship.
>
> (White, cited in Pepper 1989: 4)

Deep ecologists attempt to re-shape philosophy so as to take account of the new man/nature relation that they desire (Naess 1973). Aldo Leopold has developed a 'land ethic' that 'changes the role of *Homo sapiens* from conqueror of the land-community to plain member and citizen of it' (Leopold 1949: 239). Animal-rights theses such as that offered by Tom Regan extend the notion of moral rights to animals (Regan 1988). In all areas green political thought pursues the relation of 'man' to 'nature'. It is my contention that these debates are all made accessible, though, through an understanding of the Self/Other relation. Murray Bookchin puts it in stronger terms. For him, it is human relationships of Self to Other that provide the background to mankind's relationship to the environment:

> Ecology, in my view, has always meant social ecology: the conviction that the very concept of dominating nature stems from the domination of human by human, indeed, of women by men, of the young by their elders, of one ethnic group by another, of society by the state, of the individual by bureaucracy, as well as of one economic class by another or a colonised people by a colonial power.
>
> (Bookchin 1980: 76)

My point is slightly different: it is the argument of this chapter that the way we approach the Other accounts for relations of domination. This Other may be a human, a group of humans, a tree, 'nature'; it can be anything external to the Self in question. For instance, we think of humanity as 'us': an identifiable group with whom we feel some sense of affinity due to shared features or characteristics. Nature is different – not 'us' – external to our group. In this scenario, humanity is conceived of as an extension of Self and nature is our Other. This view of our place in the world has a long history and has been addressed by a diversity of theoretical perspectives. The following discussion is not exhaustive, but includes contributions from the fields of feminist and green political theory and psychoanalysis.

I draw upon these diverse fields of enquiry for a number of reasons. First, each in its own right represents a utopian body of thought, or at least contains utopian potentiality. Second, these different approaches, disciplines, schools, would, I suggest, do well to speak and listen to one another. Cross and interdisciplinary research is fruitful and I have argued in the previous chapters that feminism and ecologism in particular can learn from one another, methodologically and substantively. Third and more instrumentally, each of these areas addresses the Self/ Other relation. Consequently, the range of sources is diverse and includes fictional and theoretical utopias, and personal testimonies in addition to more conventional texts. In the previous chapter discussion began with material drawn from interviews and then extended into the utopian canon. Here the approach is different and the theoretical material is placed in the foreground.

Discussion is not structured by discipline or genre, but is rather divided thematically into a series of 'approaches' to this relation. The section on dualistic relations considers the account criticised by feminists, greens, psychoanalytic theory and post-structuralism: this is the historically dominant dualistic approach to Self and Other. It is familiar and, as such, requires only brief introduction. The next section focuses on approaches that identify a tension between inner fragmentation and the need for a socially cohesive sense of Self. There follows a consideration of holistic approaches that desire dissolution of the distinction of Self and Other. Heterogeneous approaches, which stress the estrangement or irreconcilability of Self and Other, are considered next. The final approach, that I describe as 'new individualism', is drawn from the testimonies and writings of people living in community at The Findhorn Foundation.

Dualistic conceptions of Self and Other

The construction of the relation of Self to Other(s) is, I suggest, historically dyadic, regardless of the number or nature of the others in question. This understanding – of Self/Other relations as dualistic and oppositional – informs all of the diverse accounts referred to below. The person, or subject, in question is self-perceived as a unit: coherent, whole and singular (both in the sense of single and unique). The Other is separate from the Self, and is in some significant way different to the Self. This view is most apparent in post-Cartesian thought, the origins of which are in René Descartes' dualistic paradigm. For Descartes, subject and object, mind and matter are distinguishable and separable:

I concluded that I was a substance whose whole essence or nature consists in thinking and whose existence depends neither on its location in space nor on any material thing.

(Descartes, *Discourse on Method*, p. 47)

Implicit in this is a hierarchy in which mind has greater value than physicality. The physical, the body in space and time, is irrelevant to Descartes' conception of himself: it is absent in his Self-understanding. It follows that creatures defined in terms of their physicality (e.g., 'animals') are fundamentally different to those characterised in terms of mind. They are different and not of equal value. Descartes continues thus:

> Thus the self, or rather the soul, by which I am what I am, is entirely distinct from the body, is indeed easier to know than the body, and would not cease to be what it is, even if there were no body.

> *(ibid.)*

Commentators link this worldview to Newtonian science (Pepper 1989: 46–50). The period between 1540–1690 is known as the scientific revolution. During this time Copernicus wrote of a heliocentric solar system (1543); Kepler worked out that planets moved according to mathematical principles (1619); Galileo evoked the language of mathematics to explain how nature worked: its movements and its composition (1623); and Newtonian physics explained gravity and motion (1687). Little wonder that mind should be privileged over matter in the contemporaneous philosophy:

> Why waste words? Geometry existed before the Creation, is co-external with the mind of God, *is God himself* (what exists in God that is not God himself?); geometry provided God with a model for the creation and was implanted into man, together with God's own likeness – and not merely conveyed to his mind through the eyes (Kepler *Harmonici Mondi*, 1619 cited in Pepper 1989: 48).

The overwhelming and awesome sense of discovery and understanding in such passages speaks to the valorisation of thought in Cartesian method. To comprehend the mechanics of the cosmos! Hardly surprising that man should be thought of as apart in some very significant way from his environment.

For Descartes, nature worked like a machine – animals also were mechanistic, having no soul and no mind. Animals, from the Latin *animalis*: 'having breath', are physical: automata. Like the universe they can be understood. What Descartes called the mind was different: not reducible.

Green political thought and feminist political thought both – albeit to different ends – focus on this period as the hatching of a previously embryonic worldview which is dualistic, hierarchical and that quite profoundly inscribes a view of 'man' as a universal subject. Man and Woman are, in this view, unequal, as are humanity and nature. Within the category of humanity are said to be several layers – at the top of which is the fully human rational autonomous subject. This subject has historically been possessed of masculine characteristics, women generally and black women in particular are associated with physicality and emotion and have been viewed as closer to nature.

Genevieve Lloyd examines this and identifies in Western philosophy a universal subject whose characteristics are masculine (Lloyd 1989). She calls this the Man of Reason. Her analysis begins with Aristotle, for whom Woman was associated with things material whilst Man embodied soul and rationality. Lloyd suggests that throughout much of our history, women (or universal Woman) have been constructed as inferior, different and Other to Man. Man is the point of reference and reason. Woman is divergent and unreasonable. Man and Woman are conceptual categories: ideal types. Lloyd finds this to be most apparent in the seventeenth-century philosophy mentioned above. Cartesian method, she says, sharpened existing prejudices and the dichotomisation of concepts becomes conventional after Descartes. Greens make a similar argument, but focus on the separation of humanity from nature. Both of these sets of analyses are critical of the paradigm that was established in this historical moment: that of dualistic and hierarchical thinking *per se*. The scientific revolution and its accompanying philosophy established a way of thinking about the world that relies on opposition of unequals and paves the way for the legitimisation of political and conceptual exclusion on a grand scale.

Some of the most interesting analysis in this field comes from contemporary feminism. Feminist theory today is increasingly preoccupied with an apparently irresolvable dilemma: the reconciliation of equality and difference. Early feminist demands for political equality are criticised from a number of contemporary perspectives. Radical and ecofeminist feminists argue that the aim for equality with men is tantamount to the desire to be like men. To be equal is to be the same, they say, and women are different to men in significant ways. Black feminism speaks also to this debate and highlights the differences amongst women, leading to the suggestion that a single feminism, which articulates the problems and desires of all women, may be inappropriate to a politics of inclusively. And French (or postmodern) feminists are concerned also with re-conceptualising difference. The point of relevance to Self and Other relations is that Self is so often identified through affinity, similarity and sameness. Self is familiar and safe, whereas the Other is seen to be different, strange, unknown and dangerous. The roles of sameness and difference in the construction of Self/Other relations are complex and will be noted at each point of the ensuing discussions. One manifestation of the association of Self with sameness and Other with difference has a direct impact on the paradigms of conceptualisation. Ariel Salleh's account is concise:

Eurocentric cultures are arranged discursively around what has standing (A) and what does not (notA). Such logic gives identity to A expressed by the value of 1. NotA is merely defined by relation to A, having no identity of its own, and thus 0 value.

(Salleh 1997: 35–6)

Salleh's substantive analysis is couched in terms of psychoanalytic feminism, to which I shall return below. First though, some introduction to psychoanalytic approaches to Self and Other relations is necessary. The point to stress for now is that this approach to the world is said to be exclusive through dualistic and hierarchical opposition.

A fragmented Self

Post-Freudian psychoanalysis tells of a sense of Self as separate from others and from the world around us. We perceive ourselves as distinct. We take ourselves as a point of reference, and we measure the world against this. For Freud, relations to the Other are governed by the libido: sexual drive, which desires the Other for its difference (Freud 1931). Lacan adds that this difference is desired for our own sense of completion (Lacan 1977). The Other is what we lack. In both of these accounts the libido is masculine, in other words, it is phallocentric: focused on desires associated with the phallus and with phallic wants. These wants are said to be for completeness, satisfaction and unilinear progress. This is sometimes explained developmentally by reference to the Freudian Oedipal complex and to the Lacanian 'mirror stage'. Both offer accounts of the ways in which a child moves into adulthood and becomes a fully functioning member of society. Both draw on the idea that we need to establish a coherently perceived self. This is done through a series of significant and difficult periods of change. Change must be successfully negotiated in order that social order (and sanity) can continue. Difference is identified as having a key role in these processes: we both desire and fear difference. The Other embodies difference and our own sense of lack.

Lacan is explicit about the role of the Other in this process. He says that the child moves from a state of undifferentiated desire into the mirror stage which gives a (false) sense of wholeness and establishes the mother as Other. In this reading the positioning of the Self, of 'I' as central in relations to others is a fundamental precondition for the development of the interacting human being. It is the perceived distinctness of the Self that appears to precipitate a privileging of identity (sameness) over difference. The Other is the person external to and different from the Self. Four things are happening here:

1 the dominance of a masculine desire;
2 the need to come to terms with this desire and to internalise it in order to become a sane and normal human adult;
3 a play of sameness and difference occurs;
4 the Other is established as the site of lack and the object of desire.

Feminists who work in this field note that masculinity approximates in complex and varying ways to men and femininity to women (Mitchell and Rose 1982). Historically, for instance, male philosophers, taking a male perspective as generically human and that of Woman as something inferior, have constructed the masculine subject of rational discourse (Shanley and Pateman 1991). Freudian psychoanalysis operates in a similar way. Freud asks: What do women want? And he then proceeds to answer for us (Freud 1977). This is not the place for full pursuit of this point, but it should be noted that psychoanalytic theory identifies masculine (superior, good and valuable) characteristics as covertly and insidiously dominant to feminine ones. Feminist theorists argue that psychoanalysis further perpetuates this (Mitchell and Rose 1982; Grosz 1990). Historically men have dominated the public sphere where these characteristics have been so highly valued and so it could be said that in this sense, masculinity and men coincide. Biologically essentialist theories of human nature reassert this. This is sometimes referred to in shorthand as culturally constructing models of Man and Woman. Man and Woman, the universal constructs, may or may not coincide with men and women, the social beings.

There is a play of sameness and difference operating here. Otherness as difference can be understood only if sameness and difference are understood as placed in an oppositional relation and can be related to the cluster of oppositions mentioned above. The utopian theory of Luce Irigaray is instructive here. In the abstract that follows, she condenses ideas of Otherness and difference in a consideration of the construction of (in this case, sexual) difference:

> 'Sexual difference' is a derivation of the problematic of sameness; it is, now and forever, determined within the project, the projection, and the sphere of representation, of the same. The 'differentiation' into two sexes derives from the a priori assumption of the same, since the little man that the girl is, must become a man minus certain attributes whose paradigm is morphological – attributes capable of determining, of assuring, the reproduction – specularization of the same. A man minus the possibility of (re)presenting oneself as a man = normal reason.
>
> (Irigaray 1990: 26–7)

Irigaray refers in this passage to the Freudian account of sexuality that takes the development of the boy child as its point of reference from which that of the girl is deviant. The progression of the girl is not the same as that of the boy; it is this difference that marks it as abnormal. Feminine sexuality is defined only in terms of its difference from masculine sexuality. Masculinity is thus equated in such accounts with normality and sameness. Difference is always difference from and is never autonomous. This may seem distant from green analysis, but the paradigm is, I suggest, the same. Irigaray, in her interrogation of sexual difference, exposes a pattern of thought which serves also to construct the human/nature relation in which humanity is Self and nature is 'our' Other. This is to take the point made by ecofeminists one stage further. Ecofeminism suggests that nature and women have a common oppressor and that this is Man, patriarchy or men – depending whom you read. Sherry Ortner articulates this in her essay which has become a classic ecofeminist text: 'Is Female to Male as Nature Is to Culture?' (Ortner 1974). The notion of shared oppression has purchase but the root, I suggest, is in the way that we think and not with specific historical agents.

Earlier I cited Ariel Shalleh's summary of the logic of negation. The passage continues thus:

> While this thought habit is not universal, it is symptomatic of a phallus-loving society which favours the eye over all other senses. Psychoanalytically, the proposition reads: since only Man has 1, he is one. When you look at Woman, by contrast, you see only 0, a hole, zero. She is thus defined negatively as lack. Woman is 'inferior', 'different', and Other. ... The same rationale of identity and difference marks the social relations of exploiters and colonisers regardless of historical context.
>
> (Salleh 1997: 35–6)

Feminist scholars of psychoanalytic theory draw the following conclusion: the Self/Other relation is constructed through binary opposition and this is normalised through the acquisition of gendered identity. Gendered identity is written into our language and we learn to behave in a way that is appropriate to a phallocentric masculinist culture as we learn to communicate through language. Language contains a symbolic order through which representation makes sense. This order was identified by Lacan as dualistic and hierarchical, being based on the negation of the Other and of femininity which is, in this tradition, Otherness: difference. All of this contributes to the subordination (variously expressed and manifested) of Woman to Man, femininity to masculinity, women to men, Nature to Humanity, Otherness to Self, difference to identity:

Masculinity	Femininity
Man	Woman
Men	Women
Humanity	Nature
Self	Otherness
Identity	Difference

A fundamentally fragmented Self is given a sense of coherence through the paradigm of binary opposition, which drives the Symbolic Order.

Slightly different in its politics is the field of social psychology. The work of Herbert Mead is canonical here. His social psychology draws also on a dualistic notion of Self and Other. Mead wrote in the 1930s, in the context of fascist ascendancy. He is associated with American pragmatism, alongside John Dewey. This may account for his affection for reason and his social psychology differs from that of Freud in part in its stress on the rational side of human behaviour. Mead attempts to account for the construction of a social sense of 'me' that co-exists with the internal but also constructed 'I'. In *Mind, Self, and Society* (1934), he takes an approach which is rooted in a focus on the individual, but which assumes this individual to be part of something larger: a social order.

> If we abandon the conception of a substantive soul endowed with the self of the individual at birth, then we may regard the development of the individual's self, and of his self-consciousness within the field of his experience, as the social psychologist's special interest.
>
> (Mead, 1934: 128)

This approach combines attention to physiology and socialisation. His method is described as 'social behaviourism'. It is accessible, being less technical than psychoanalytic accounts. Of interest to the current enquiry though is the fact that all of Mead's accounts of the construction of the Self assume the pre-existence of an external and larger Other, against whom character formation and social role are constructed. The Other, in other words, is a point of reference and opposition. He begins by stating that the individual is incomprehensible outside of 'his' context:

> Social psychology studies the activity or behaviour of the individual as it lies within the social process; the behaviour of the individual can be understood only in terms of the behaviour of the whole social group of which he is a member, since his individual acts are involved in larger, social acts which go beyond himself and which implicate the other members of the group.
>
> (Mead, 1934: 133)

An example of such acts is the use of socially significant gestures in communication. Mead is interesting on this. He also posits a dynamic model of the construction of the Self; the Self is not a 'given', inscribed at birth, but rather develops in a context. Dualisms of nurture and nature, individual and society are negotiated. The Self is formed in a process of interaction with others. The Self is, he says, separate from the body, and here Mead continues the tradition referred to above, of separation of mind or essence (spirit) from body.

> We can distinguish very definitely between the self and the body. The body can be there and can operate in a very intelligent fashion without there being a self involved in the experience. The self has the characteristic that it is an object to itself and that characteristic distinguishes it from other objects and from the body.
>
> (Mead, 1934)

This separation is only possible if the body and mind are conceived of as separate, and it is to this that deep ecological accounts are opposed. Feminist accounts also challenge this assumption (Sargisson 1996: 133–69). Within dualistic thought there has always to be an Other for things to make sense.

The Other is the secondary partner in the dualism. It is needed, for without it nothing would be communicable, but it is devalued because dualistic thought works through opposition and hierarchy. Suppose, for instance, that the way we think about the world, and the way we make sense of the world is informed by a dualism that opposes mind to body and spirit to matter. Mind, in the tradition mentioned above, has been privileged over body – mind it is assumed can conquer body, can know body and can dominate body. Access to God and to higher states of being is through the exercise of spirit: our 'higher' self. Access to knowledge and to the truths of the Universe is through the exercise of the mind. Now suppose, as feminist accounts would have it, that women have historically been associated with the body and matter and men with the mind and spirit. Or, alternatively (additionally, in some accounts), that nature has been associated with body and matter and humanity with mind and spirit. It is a way of constructing the world that facilitates some fundamental inequalities and exclusions.

> We who are born into this civilisation have inherited a habit of mind. We are divided against ourselves ... To us the word *thought* means an activity separate from feeling, just as the word *mind* suggests a place apart from the body and from the rhythms of the earth ... Through the words *masculine* and *feminine*, which we use to designate two alien and alienated poles of human behaviour, we make our sexuality a source of separation. We divide ourselves and all that we know along an invisible border between what we call Nature and what we believe is superior to Nature.
>
> (Griffin 1989: 7–8)

For Mead, the Other is essential to the process of self-knowledge. Reason facilitates self-consciousness and allows us to take an 'objective view' of ourselves (*ibid.*: 215). This, however, occurs only with an awareness of the perceptions of others:

> The individual perceives himself as such, not directly, but only indirectly, from the particular standpoints of other individual members of the same social group, or from the generalised standpoint of the social group as a whole to which he belongs ... he becomes an object to himself only by taking the attitudes of other individuals toward himself within a social environment or context of experience and behaviour in which both he and they are involved.
>
> (Mead, 1934: 215–16)

It is at this point that the social 'me' is formed. Only once this social Self has been formed can we think of ourselves as a solitary and isolated 'I'. The social Self is not fixed and can vary according to context. There are, he says, all sorts of different social selves that can operate simultaneously in most people. All depend though on context; on externalities; on others. Mead presents this in terms of social process:

> The unity and structure of the complete self reflects the unity and structure of the social process as a whole; and each of the elementary selves of which it is composed reflects a unity and structure of one of the various aspects of that process in which the individual is implicated ... the structure of the complete self is thus a reflection of the complete social process.
>
> The organised community or social group which gives to the individual his unity of self may be called the 'generalised other'. The attitude of the generalised other is the attitude of the whole community.
>
> (*ibid.*: 221, 231)

I do not propose to spend longer with Mead but wish only to note the dynamics of his approach. Whilst resistant to gross simplifications regarding the individual and society and whilst subtle in this respect, his method is driven nonetheless by a dualistic approach which dates beyond its fullest articulation in the Cartesian method.

Psychoanalytic accounts of Self and Other are useful as descriptive accounts. So is that of social psychology. Feminists working in these fields though have shown them to re-affirm the exclusionary structures that they identify. For instance, Freud's account of teenage sexuality in 'The Dora case' is useful. It identifies some of the paradoxes of adolescence. Dora is taken to Freud by her parents as an aphonic hysteric. She is not a willing patient. Freud draws lasting lessons out of her story. She is treated simultaneously as a child and an adult: she is given responsibility beyond her years, and she is babied. She is empowered (by the adult roles that her family ask her to assume) and dis-empowered ('She's only a child!' says the man who has been sexually abusing her). In this way, the separation of childhood from adulthood is problematised by Freud. But also, and at the same time, he re-affirms a dualistic notion of gender as he tells her story (Sargisson 1996). This feminist analogy may seem tangential but, as suggested above, these analyses of the Self and Other relation (as dualistically gendered) speak to the same paradigm that constructs humanity as opposing (and superior to) nature. Humanity and nature are concepts, constructs, as are gender and sexuality, and as are Self and Other. A core element in green political thought is the 'holistic' assertion that the root of a problem should be addressed prior to addressing its symptoms. In this, I think, they have a point. The construction of Self/Other relations is complex and difficult. It raises many issues and no single discipline can, I suggest, claim ownership of its resolution.

Holistic conceptions of Self and Other

Green political thought in general and 'deep ecology' in particular conceives of Self and Other in symbiosis: interconnectedness and interdependence are key terms here. The work of Arne Naess has to be our starting point as it is to this that all ecological accounts eventually refer (Humphrey, 1999). Naess wrote his short but influential account of deep green ecology in the early 1970s. Published as 'The shallow and the deep: Long-range ecology movement', this essay has canonical status. It has been fleshed out since, but the essence of Naess's 'ecosophy' has remained constant:

1   Rejection of the man-in-environment image in favour of the relational, total-field image.
2   Biospherical egalitarianism – in principle.
3   Principles of diversity and symbiosis.
4   Anti-class posture.
5   Fight against pollution and resource depletion.
6   Complexity, not complication.
7   Local autonomy and decentralisation.

(Naess 1973: 95–9)

Deep ecology rejects the dualistic paradigm that constructs an anthropocentric worldview in which 'man' is in opposition to 'nature'. Instead, holism permits it to be ecocentric.

A number of things about Naess' approach are noteworthy before proceeding to the specifics of his ontology. In Chapter 3 'Publicising the private', I stated that one implication of feminist interventions in the terrain of the political is that emotions are introduced into public political discourse. Intuition has a special role in much feminist thought where it is valorised alongside – or in the place of – rationality and reasoned debate (Daly 1979; Jagger 1989). Green political thought also privileges intuition, and in Naess' later work this is given full expression. Naess writes of having lived in close connection with nature and of intuiting another relationship with the natural. Intuition is offered without apology as the source of knowledge and as the route to understanding Naess' position. The reader of *Ecology, Community, and Lifestyle* is invited to suspend disbelief and see whether the book feels right:

> Is not the value-laden, spontaneous and emotional realm of experience as genuine a source of knowledge of reality as mathematical physics?
>
> (Naess 1989: 32)

Warwick Fox, whose *Towards a Transpersonal Ecology* also occupies canonical status, makes similar claims for the role of emotions and intuition. For Fox, the transpersonal theory of self that he develops is self-evident: we will simply realise it to be more true and authentic than the tripartite theory of self to which he contrasts it. Freya Mathews, in her *The Ecological Self*, adopts a more rationalistic style than Naess or Fox, but also insists on a non-objective realisation of her intuition in her text (Humphrey 1999). Of the monistic theory of substance for instance, in which 'all is thought to be one', she says the following:

It always seemed plain to me, intuitively; that the way we conceived of reality and our place in the scheme of things was central to questions about the meaning and the ends of life.

This was an intuitive belief in which I already had a strong emotional investment. It seemed to me ethically and aesthetically satisfying and 'right'.

(Mathews 1991: 1–2)

These points of method are derived from an ecological affection for the restoration of balance and wholeness. This, it is argued, has been damaged by the dualistic thought of Western religion and philosophy. Introducing 'the feminine' into masculinist discourse; and introducing neglected human characteristics into our thinking about our environment, are thought to be ways of redressing imbalance and restoratives to the perceived 'ills' of philosophical rationalism.

Naess' conception of the relation of Self and Other aims similarly at healing and restoration of wholeness. Instead of opposing Self to external and unknown Other, Naess proposes a conceptual widening of Self to include the Other. He presents this in terms of man's relationship with nature. If, he says, we can accomplish this conceptual shift, we can then think of nature as a part of ourselves. To harm nature then is to harm a part of us.

At the heart of Naess' work on the relationship between human and non-human is 'Self-Realisation'. This is a self-improving and dynamic process which, he says, is an essential part of the shift in consciousness necessary to found a sustainable future. As such it is part of his utopian vision, intuitively imminent. The status of the concept is made clear:

the term 'Self-Realisation' is used to indicate a kind of perfection. It is conceived as a process, but also as an ultimate goal, in a rather special usage of 'ultimate'. It is logically ultimate in a systematic exposition of Ecosophy T.

(Naess 1989: 84)

There is, within utopian studies, debate regarding utopianism and perfectionism. I have referred to this in the previous chapters. Briefly, utopias, for a long time, were assumed to be articulations of political desire (Levitas 1990), which were thought by their creators to be perfectible (Goodwin 1978; Davies 1981). This accounts for two historical criticisms of the utopia: its impossible idealism and, more compelling, its totalitarian tendencies. Latterly it has been argued that utopias are not necessarily literal blueprints for the perfect world. Rather, it is suggested, they can also be usefully conceived of as visions that encourage a change in perspective (Sargisson 1996), a process (Bammer 1991) and speak to a critical mass of political opposition, thereby contributing to social and political transformation (Moylan 1986). Commentators who focus on perfection as a defining characteristic of utopia read this phenomenon as static and finite. Those who are more interested in utopia as part of a process of change focus on its dynamism and ambiguity. Naess combines a utopian desire for the realisation of perfection with affection for utopia as process.

The content of Self-Realisation hovers between a Liberal utopia of the self-improving citizen of the world, and a religious (pagan?) vision of spiritual inter-connection. Consciousness of Self expands, in this approach, to embrace the Other:

> The term includes personal and communal self-realisation, but is conceived also to refer to an unfolding of reality as a totality ... it asks for the develop-ment of a deep identification of individuals with all life forms.
>
> (*ibid.*: 84–5)

Naess asks for a radical shift in consciousness. The lived reality of such a shift would be naturally harmonious. It would lead us away from moral teaching to greater introspection – we would not need to be told to care for our environ-ment, we would need only to look inwardly and we would 'know' that we ought to care for it as part of ourselves. This, he says, is benevolence and ben-evolence is a part of human maturation.

Naess creates what is undoubtedly a transgressive utopian concept here. It is transgressive of the division of Self from Other which, it is suggested, dominates Western philosophy. He sees this mindset as contributing to alienation, separation and, ultimately, Self-negation and as being profoundly destructive in ecosophical terms (*ibid.*: 172). His ideal, Self-Realisation, is offered both as a critique and an alternative to this way of thinking about the world. Behavioural change is sustain-able, he implies, only when grounded by a change in the way that we think. In all of these senses then the work of Naess typifies the kind of utopianism privileged by this book. Further, his method, which includes emotions in theoretical discourse, might seem also to exemplify the kind of approach argued for in earlier chapters.

There is indeed a certain lightness of touch employed, which seeks to avoid closure and to allow for diversity even within the process of conceptualisation. Naess' new ontology – his new way of knowing the world – has within it unin-scribed space that retains utopian potentiality. David Rothenberg, Naess' transla-tor, describes this as follows:

> A word only takes life through its meanings and compatible interpretations. This is the practical effect of realising ecosophical ontology. We can only etch out the meaning of a concept through its moving place in the field of other concepts and the ways they are perceived.
>
> (Rosenberg in Naess 1989: 6)

However, two elements of Naess's work require further exploration. One is the tendency in the philosophy of deep ecology to privilege emotion and intuition to the neglect of their traditional counterparts: rationality and reason. Inversion of hierarchy is not, I suggest, sufficient to challenge the existence of hierarchy *per se*. The underprivileged becomes the dominant party and the hierarchical and dualistic mindset continues. On the level of method then, or approach, Naess's approach is problematic. Further, in terms of the content of his new relation of Self and Other nothing authentically original is offered. The expansion of Self to include deep and intuitive knowledge of Other is not a shift in the fundamental separation of Self and Other at all. Rather it is a massive assertion of Self, and of sameness, which serves merely to deny the Other its difference. With such a huge sense of self, what space is there for Otherness?

Naess might defend himself thus: Ecosophy T, which is his ecosophy (we are invited to develop our own), does not negate difference but rather it embraces it. Self-Realisation is not an expansion of an isolated and egotistical Self. It does not do violence to the Other. It does not negate the Other.

It is nonetheless based on affinity and identity and on the belief that it is possible to know the Other, to be intimate with the Other. It assumes ontological access to the Other. This is problematic.

> By identifying with greater wholes, we partake in the creation and maintenance of this whole. *We thereby share in its greatness.* . . . The egos develop into selves of greater dimension, proportional to the extent and depth of our process of identification.
>
> (*ibid.*: 174)

All forms of life have an equal 'right' to this realisation of Self:

> The right of all the forms to live is a universal right that cannot be quantified. No single species of living being has more of this particular right to live and unfold than any other species.
>
> (*ibid.*: 166)

This is what Naess calls 'biospherical egalitarianism – in principle' (1973: 95). His theory of Self-Realisation is not confined to the human being, but is, in principle, equally valid for all forms of life. Life has intrinsic value in this account and this intuited 'fact' is the grounding for the egalitarianism application of this 'right'. This is, of course, curious. The use of intuition in this way is of suspect value and lends itself to mysticism and is unassailable. No philosophy should ever be so certain of itself as to have no need for analytic defence. This is a result of Naess' methodological inversion of rationality and emotion. A theory grounded solely in one or the other of these things is, I suggest, bound to be exclusive and to impose unnecessary closure on debate.

Naess' approach does, however, allow space for manoeuvre within the concept of Self. It privileges process over blueprint, and it is not self-centred in exactly the same way as is the liberal capitalist Self. Naess invites us to expand our sense of Self and to root ourselves in our environment, which is part of us and which we know and love as part of ourselves. All of these traits in his approach point towards it being a critical utopia in the sense established by Tom Moylan (Moylan 1986). I hesitate though to offer this as an example of a transgressive utopia because I am not convinced that Naess succeeds in undermining the paradigms that structure currently dominant Self/Other relations. It is still ontology based on affection for sameness. It is still one that privileges Self. It could be argued that Otherness, radical difference, disappears in Naess's utopia, as the world becomes intimately and intuitively knowable.

If Naess gestures in this direction, then other deep ecologists gallop towards it headlong. Warwick Fox's account of ecologism attributes to it a utopian function:

> this approach attempts to foster a greater awareness of the intimate and manifold relationships that exist between what we conventionally designate as *self* and what we conventionally designate as *environment*. It attempts, in other words, to foster the development of an *ecological* rather than *environmental* consciousness.
>
> (Fox 1990: 8)

Fox draws here on the now classical distinction between ecologism (deep green ecocentric) and environmentalism (shallow and anthropocentric). The ecologist analysis of Self and Other attempts, he says, to change the way that we think: to provoke a shift in consciousness. It is implied that this shift is of a paradigmatic nature. Deep ecology argues that environmentalism is not sufficient for sustainable change: technological fixes are not appropriate unless accompanied by a shift in the way that we think about our relationship to our environment. Human self-importance, says Fox sweepingly, has 'been the single deepest and most persistent assumption of (at least) all the *dominant* western philosophical, social, and political traditions since the time of the classical Greeks' (*ibid*.: 9).

Fox proposes a 'transpersonal' theory of Self. He stresses that this is not 'cross-personal', not, in other words, anthropocentric but rather one that transcends the individual and the division of humanity from nature. His starting point is the work of Naess and echoes of this can be heard in Fox's proclamations:

> a transpersonal approach to ecology is concerned primarily with *opening* to ecological awareness; with realising one's ecological, wider, or big Self; or, ... with the this-worldly realisation of as expansive a sense of self as possible.
>
> (*ibid*.: 198)

This has credence in New Age circles and I shall refer to it again below in consideration of the 'New Individualistic Self'. Briefly though, Fox draws upon a popular psychology called transpersonal theory. His version is, he claims, unique because it is not anthropocentric. Transpersonal theory takes a tripartite theory of the human Self (desire and impulse; rationalising and deciding; and normative and judgmental). These three versions of Self co-exist in most individuals and are associated respectively with behaviour that is childlike, adult, and 'higher' or transcendent. Echoes of Plato and Rousseau have resonance. Transpersonal theory is hierarchical: the transcendent Self is 'better' than is the childlike Self. If the enlightened higher Self can be encouraged to prevail, says Fox, then ethics are rendered superfluous. Naess made a similar claim: there is no need for systems of morals or rules or codes of behaviour if we can follow our enlightened 'natures', we will simply do well intuitively (Naess 1989). A shift in consciousness is all that is required:

> The reason for this is that if one has a wide, expansive, or field-like sense of self then (assuming that one is not self-destructive) one will naturally (i.e. spontaneously) protect the natural (spontaneous) unfolding of this expansive self (the ecosphere, the cosmos) in all its aspects.
>
> (Fox 1990: 217)

Simple!

Identification is at the centre of Fox's approach to the Other. The widening and deepening of the Self is, he says, achievable through identification with our environment. He is keen to stress that this identification is not a process that results in homogenisation.

> Identification should be taken to mean what we ordinarily mean by that term, that is, the experience not simply of a sense of *similarity* with an entity but a sense of *commonality*. ... What identification should not be taken to mean, however, is *identity* – that I literally *am* that tree over there, for example.
>
> (*ibid.*: 231)

Nonetheless, commonality – shared experience – grounds this shift in consciousness. Fox invites us to open our minds and think about what we already intuit, but neglect to notice: that we are connected experientially to, say, 'that tree over there'. Presumably we can achieve this by realising that the tree is also a victim of pollution, of environmental degradation, as well as being part of our ecosphere and a provider of oxygen. It is living and has inherent worth. It is part of us as we are part of it, in experiential terms. What is interesting about this approach is that it breaks the connection between Otherness and danger. Here the source of danger, presumably, is the Self, or rather humanity of which we are a part.

> What is being emphasised is the tremendously *common* experience that through the process of identification my *sense* of self (my experiential self) can expand to include the tree even though I and the tree remain physically separate.
>
> (*ibid.*: 232)

This is slippery. The tree both is and is not separate from me – I am not the tree, but I am supposed to experience commonality with the tree.

Identification is not identity, but a sense of identity (knowledge of the Other) is necessary in order to achieve a sense of commonality. The commonality suggested by Fox is not one of mere empiricism, but contains reference to knowledge of metaphysical states of being. Fox seems oblivious here to questions of agency and responsibility – I, for instance, can take a chainsaw to the tree, and I am already partially responsible for its pollution. My habits of consumption make this so. This is not an equitable relationship. I do not experience the tree's degradation: I cause it. There is, I suggest an invisible Other that is the 'baddy' of Fox's tale: other human beings that are less enlightened than me. Others inflict violence upon the tree and me and we unite here in our victimhood. The ontological claim underlying Fox's transpersonal ecology is spurious. Ontology grounded in commonality should, surely, note that humans have a greater commonality of experience with each other than they do with 'nature'. He implies this himself in the following appeal to common-sense empiricism:

> This is the way in which most of us think of the process of identification most of the time. We generally tend to identify most with the entities with which we are often in contact (assuming our experiences of these entities are of a generally positive kind). [he gives the examples of football teams, families, nation] We experience these entities as part of 'us' as part of our identity. An assault on their integrity is an assault upon our integrity.
>
> (*ibid.*: 249–50)

The type of thinking advocated here is not significantly transgressive of the oppositional Self/Other relation. Rather it is a subsumption of Otherness. This is not dissimilar to the worldview that permits cultural imperialism – it allows us authority to speak for the Other: to represent the Other.

Deep ecological approaches to the Self/Other relation are surely utopian, but not perhaps in a wholly unproblematic sense. Utopianism has its dark sides. It has totalitarian potential. There are dangers in an appeal to intuition and 'gut' feelings. There are dangers in assuming total access to the Other – especially such a large and generalised Other as 'the environment': dangers of misrepresentation and appropriation.

In order to make these points more clearly I shall turn now to the penultimate utopian body for consideration. This is variously described as post-modern and post-structuralist and though these terms are cumbersome and alienating I shall employ them for want of a better alternative.

Heterogeneous Self–Other relations

The accounts referred to in this section share the following features: they come from a tradition which is critical of binary oppositional thought; they believe language to be in some way constitutive of experiences of reality; and they identify property to be the dynamic of Self/Other relations. Further, they are attentive to the relationship of sameness and difference. I have argued elsewhere that they also share a certain utopianism and that this is a good thing. Briefly, I have suggested that their utopianism: the utopian moments that occur in their analyses, permit something other than the nihilism for which postmodernism is infamous (Sargisson 1996). It permits the facilitation of thinking that is significantly different to that of which they are critical.

One of the clearest expositions of this critique of Self/Other relations comes, surprisingly, from Jean Baudrillard. (Surprising because Baudrillard is not renowned for accessibility.) In a collection of essays published in translation as *The Transparency of Evil* (1993), Baudrillard explores what he terms 'the hell of the same', the 'melodrama of difference' and other routes towards what he terms 'irreconcilability'. His approach is oblique and his critique focuses on cloning, psychodrama and other bizarre contemporary phenomena. The substance of his critique is familiar: the human subject is situated in a symbolic order of relationships that privileges sameness and which inflicts both violence and negation onto the Other. This, he says, is obvious:

> To master the universal symbols of Otherness and difference is to master the world. Those who conceptualise difference are anthropologically superior – naturally, because it is they who invented anthropology. They have all the rights, because rights, too, are their invention.
>
> (Baudrillard 1993: 133)

In order fully to comprehend this we need some understanding of theory of property in contemporary politico-linguistic theory. Put simply, theories of language that draw on post-structuralism see the act of naming (defining, describing and the ascription of characteristics) to be part of a process in which power is exercised.

The work of Jacques Derrida forms a useful point of entry into these debates. Derrida, to whom the tags 'post-structuralist', 'anti-philosopher' and 'postmodernist' are variously and carelessly ascribed, has developed an approach to writing known as 'deconstruction'. Derrida draws upon an eclectic range of sources, which include the work of Freud, Lacan, Saussure, Neitzsche and Levinas (of whom more on p. 138). From Freudian psychoanalysis he draws the concepts of libidinal economies. These were mentioned on pp. 122–23. From Lacan comes the idea that these are two, and they are gendered: the masculine being dominant, the feminine being the unknown and representing Otherness. These are economies of cultural and social exchange: they form the informal structures that mediate our relations with Others.

> Essentially and lawfully, every concept is inscribed in a chain or system within which it refers to the other, to other concepts, by means of the systematic play of differences.
>
> (Derrida 1972: 36)

It is the word 'concept' or 'conception' that I would in turn question in its relation to any essence which is rigorously or properly identifiable. ... The concept of the concept, along with the entire system that attends it, belongs to a prescriptive order.

(Derrida 1982: 448)

Concepts inhabit a system – or economy, the function of which is the creation of meaning. Meaning is thus codified. He names these economies 'The Proper' and 'The Gift'. The Proper is dominant. The Gift is utopian, unattainable and even unimaginable.[2] For Derrida, the Drive of the Proper dominates the way that we currently think about the world and our place in it. This is a conflation of all senses of the word 'property', and was referred to in the previous chapter.

Derrida writes of a 'cultural text'. This is shorthand for the way that language is thought to inscribe our individual psyches or consciousness. Thus, we are said to be 'written', even as we write. There is, he says, nothing outside of the text and it is this that makes thinking about a Gift economy so difficult. Within an economy driven by the desire to appropriate, the act of speaking is politically inscribed. Naming is claiming power. It is an activity in which the named is denied autonomy. The possibility of conceptuality is, in this critique, a profound expression of the possibility of naming, which is enclosing and restricting. This is due in part to the closure invoked by acts of definition. Definitions exclude, that is their function. The point made by post-structuralists (and feminists) is that often the exclusion is unnecessary or unjust. The repressed Other has no space for self-expression in such a system.

Baudrillard displays, with characteristic flamboyance, a sense of boredom with this situation. Speaking in negative terms of utopia as an impossible goal, he characterises the model of (sexual) difference produced by such a paradigm as utopian:

> One sex is never the other of the other sex, except within the context of a differentialistic theory of sexuality – which is basically nothing but a utopia. *For difference is itself a utopia*: the idea that such pairs of terms can be split up is a dream – and the idea of subsequently reuniting them is another. ... Only in the distinction-based perspective of our culture is it possible to speak of the Other in connection with sex. Genuine sexuality ... resides in the radical incomparability of the sexes – otherwise seduction would be never be possible, and there would be nothing but alienation of one sex by the other.
>
> (Baudrillard 1993: 128)

The last sentence of this statement asserts a characteristic desire for 'pure' difference. Variously phrased in 'post-modern' analyses as radical difference,

---

2 Feminist theorists Luce Irigaray and Helene Cixous have radicalised these economies to feminist ends.

radical Otherness, incommensurability and alterity, this difference is a difference that is not reducible to the same. Or, more accurately, it is an approach to (Otherness) difference which does not seek to reduce it to a counterpart of the (Self) same. For Baudrillard, this pure Otherness is not politically exclusive:

> Racism does not exist so long as the other remains other, so long as the Stranger remains foreign. It comes into existence when the other becomes merely different – that is to say, dangerously similar. This is the moment when the inclination to keep the other at a distance comes into being.
>
> (*ibid.*: 129)

This response could not be more different to the all-consuming total-field consciousness desired by deep ecologists. There, the desire was for intimacy and knowledge – an expansion of Self to encompass all Others. This was a consuming Self. Here, strangeness is desired for its own sake. The exotic, for Baudrillard, is the exciting, the object of desire – but not a devouring desire that robs its object of autonomy and identity. In an essay 'Radical exoticism', he is unusually hopeful:

> The very scale of the efforts made to exterminate the Other is testimony to the Other's indestructibility, and by extension to the indestructible totality of Otherness.
>
> Radical otherness survives everything: conquest, racism, extermination, the virus of difference, the psychodrama of alienation. On the one hand, the Other is always-already dead; on the other hand, the Other is indestructible.
>
> (*ibid.*: 146)

In this way, Baudrillard asserts the tenacity of irreducible difference. This is why I claim this approach to be utopian. Not only is it critical – but also in this work is an assertion that the order that currently structures relations is not inevitable. Not, in other words, watertight and seamless. One common criticism of this approach is that it writes itself into a state of frozen immobility: it denies the possibility of things ever being any different It is said to be eternally pessimistic, if not nihilistic. Students studying this often say, triumphantly: 'If they're right, then how can we begin to think differently, if our language forms the way that we think?' Baudrillard's simple denial of triumph to the approach that negates difference is one way of negotiating this apparent void. It permits a utopian space to exist, a new no place in which it may be possible to imagine another way of approaching the world. In this place we let go of the quest for understanding and encounter irreducible difference *per se*:

> True knowledge is knowledge of exactly what we can never understand in the other, knowledge of what it is in the other that makes the other not

oneself – and hence someone who can in no sense become separated from oneself, nor alienated by any look of ours, nor instituted by us in either identity or difference.

The Other is what allows me not to repeat myself for ever.

(ibid.: 148, 174)

Other thinkers take more or less sophisticated approaches, but the hallmark is an assertion of 'pure' difference. The most original thinker on the relationship of Self and Other is the Judaic scholar, Emmanuel Levinas. Levinas' approach to the relation of Self and Other is not dualistic, nor fragmentary, nor holistic. It is quite profoundly utopian, in the sense of that word used throughout this book. It attempts to foresee an unforeseeable relation of Self and Other, to inscribe onto our consciousness something entirely other to that ordained by our culture and traditions of philosophy. However, it does not attempt to close the loop: utopia, as the vision of Otherness, remains uninscribed – almost.

Levinas stands accused of misogynism (at worst), gender blindness (at best), mysticism and wilful inaccessibility (de Beauvior; Derrida). Most of these accusations are sustainable, but there is nonetheless tremendous power in his work on Self and Other. Levinas claims to draw upon Husserlian phenomenology, which focuses on lived experience as the source of meaningful knowledge (see, e.g., Husserl in Cahoone 1996). His search though is not for scientific knowledge, and he gives to his claims a metaphysical status. In *Totality and Infinity* (1969), he rejects the totalising claims for knowledge made by the 'western tradition' of philosophy, preferring instead to defer such claims, holding forever open the possibility of meaning: hence 'infinity'. Some attention to context is important here. Levinas wrote and delivered his lectures as a Jew in the immediate wake of the Holocaust. The lectures later published as *Time and the Other* (1979) were, for instance, delivered in France in 1946 and 1947. By this time, it had become apparent to many that Self/Other relations had been lived and died for. Rethinking these relations was not a mental exercise, not an apolitical game, but was something deadly earnest.

> Many people – many nations – can find themselves holding, more or less wittingly, that 'every stranger is an enemy'. For the most part this conviction lies deep down like some latent infection; it betrays itself only in random, disconnected acts, and does not lie at the base of a system of reason. But when this does come about, when the unspoken dogma becomes the premise in a syllogism, then, at the end of the chain, there is the Lager. Here is the product of a conception of the world carried rigorously to its logical conclusion; so long as the conception subsists, the conclusion remains to threaten us.
>
> (Primo Levi 1979: 15)

The struggle with Levinas' difficult texts is worthwhile. He begins *Time and the Other* with mediation of pain and suffering. Through suffering, he says, we engage unequivocally in existence. Suffering permits us to accomplish solitude, for pain is a solitary state that no one else can know or share. He refers, I think, to physical pain, and imagines pain as a place in which we can be in anguish and whence we can cry out to others, but they cannot join us there. We can try to describe our pain, but they cannot share it. This is unknowable. Pain, he says, is proximate to death: 'Death is the end of suffering' (Levinas 1989: 40). Death is the finish of suffering, and the end towards which it takes us. Death is ultimate. Death is also a moment at which something incredible may occur: a new relation to the Other:

> Consequently only a being whose solitude has reached a crispation through suffering, and in relation with death, takes its place on a ground where the relation with the other becomes possible.
>
> (*ibid.*: 43)

Throughout these lectures, he draws on a motif that recurs in his work: that of light. Light, for Levinas, is a metaphor for understanding. He is critical of this as an approach to the world. Light illuminates. This works well in English translation as the Latin word *lucis* informs the etymology of both 'light' and 'learning'. For Levinas, illumination: understanding, is not innocent, and is profoundly self-referential:

> The light, brightness, is intelligibility itself; making everything come from me, it reduces every experience to an element of reminiscence.
>
> (Levinas in Hand 1989: 39)

The political import of this is its direct relevance to the way in which we think of Self and Other. Readers in English translation can find clues to this in the word 'comprehend' and in Levinas' play on the word 'grasp'. The words are etymologically linked, and Levinas claims that our history of learning and understanding has been one in which knowledge has been grasped: grabbed hold and taken close to the Self. This can be phrased in terms of property relations and we could say that the quest for knowledge has been acquisitive. Knowledge claims become appropriative of power. This becomes clear when Levinas poses his alternative relation with the Other:

> The relationship with the other will never be the feat of grasping a possibility. One would have to characterise it in terms that contrast strongly with the relationships that describe light.
>
> (*ibid.*: 43)

Against the motif of light he sets the unknowable depths of death. Further consideration of this is, perhaps, necessary as a preliminary to meeting the Other on Levinas' terms.

It is not with the nothingness of death, of which we know precisely nothing, that the analysis must begin, but with the situation where something absolutely unknowable appears. Absolutely unknowable means foreign to all light, rendering every assumption of possibility impossible, but where we are ourselves seized.

(*ibid.*: 41)

In 'Substitution', he makes his position clear. In our tradition of thought, he says (which is to say one that is driven by the desire for self-security and safety), we meet the Other like this:

> To be conscious of a being is then always for that being to be grasped across an ideality and on the basis of a said. ... The detour of ideality leads to co-inciding with oneself, that is, to a certainty, which remains the guide and guarantee of the whole spiritual adventure. But this is why this adventure is no adventure. It is never dangerous; it is self-possession, sovereignty, ... Anything unknown that can occur is cast in the mould of the known, and cannot be a complete surprise.
>
> (Levinas, 'Substitution', in Hand 1989: 89)

This assertion recurs in his work. In 'Ethics as first responsibility' he says the following of Aristotle's *Metaphysics*:

> Here, the known is understood and so *appropriated* by knowledge, and as it were *freed* of its otherness. In the realm of truth, being as the *other* of thought becomes the characteristic *property* of thought as knowledge. ... But in knowledge there also appears the notion of an intellectual activity or of a reasoning will – a way of doing something which consists of thinking through knowing, of seizing something and making it one's own, of reducing presence and representing the difference of being, an activity which *appropriates* and *grasps* the otherness of the known. A certain grasp: as an entity, being becomes the characteristic property of thought, as it is grasped by it and becomes known.
>
> (Levinas, 'Ethics as first philosophy', in Hand 1989: 76)

This describes a relation with the Other that permits no Otherness: no difference. The desire for security quashes the space occupied by the Other, which becomes filled with a version of us. This is a safe way of relating to the Other. It takes no risks. It leads us back to the Self and thus reassures us of our sovereignty. It is such a seductive way of relating to the Other that it looks like a closed system: it looks inevitable. Against this, I suggest, we need spaces where something new and/or different might be conceivable. This is why I describe Levinas' approach to death as utopian.

Death and that which we encounter in death are, for Levinas, symbolic of an ultimate Otherness. In this sense, I suggest, he treats death as a utopic space. A space: a place, in which the codes and rules of our present are not applicable.

They are transgressed and rendered meaningless. Light and illumination have literally no place here. Further, it is a utopian construct because it is a place in which the unforeseeable can be encountered. However, I accept that this may seem a peculiar utopia. What happens to the subject at the point of death is overwhelming to and of 'us'.

> This approach of death indicates that we are in relation with something that is absolutely other, something bearing alterity not as a provisional determination we can assimilate through enjoyment, but as something whose very existence is made up of alterity.
>
> (Levinas, 'Time and the Other', in Hand 1989: 43)

The presence indicated could, I suggest, be interpreted as a deity or simply as death itself. The Other, he says '... is not unknown but unknowable, refractory to all light' (*ibid*.: 43). Relations with this Other are not relations of communion or intimacy and there is no commonality between us:

> The Other's entire being is constituted by its exteriority, or rather its alterity, for exteriority is a property of space and leads the subject back to itself through light.
>
> (*ibid*.: 43)

It is not death itself that I find utopian here, but rather Levinas' conceptualisation of death. Death itself is not utopian: it denies agency to the seer, the person who envisages and desires. Creativity is not permitted in this place. It is, further, an ironic utopia as death is one thing of which we can, phenomenologically, be assured – yet against which we struggle. Death works well in Levinas as a metaphor for a place in which conceptuality is impossible, it is a place that we cannot know but that we will experience. In one short line, he undermines his own metaphor: 'Suicide is a contradictory concept' (*ibid*.: 42). And so death contains its own internal transgression of itself: its own meaning and status. A further irony exists here because only in suicide: the ultimate self-destruction, is the subject permitted agency. Only in this act of transgression can one assert one's will. He speaks of death as the 'limit of the subject's virility', and 'the loss of mastery as a subject' (*ibid*.: 42). This, he says, is why we struggle against it.

A further motif in Levinas' work is that of the face. The face greets us. It reveals and conceals the Other. He describes this:

> The proximity of the other is the face's meaning, and it means from the very start in a way that goes beyond those plastic forms which forever try to cover the face like a mask of their presence and perception. But always the face shows through these forms. Prior to any particular expression and beneath all particular expressions, which cover over and protect with an immediately adopted face or countenance, there is the nakedness and

destitution of the expression as such, that is to say extreme exposure, defence-lessness, vulnerability itself.

(Levinas, 'Ethics and responsibility' in Hand, 1989: 82–3)

The face resists possession, resists my powers. In its epiphany, in expression, the sensible, still graspable, turns into total resistance to the grasp. ... The expression the face introduces into the world does not deny the feebleness of my powers, but my ability for power.

(Levinas 1969: 197)

This naked and vulnerable face is phenomenologically there: present. It confronts us and compels us. Death and mortality reside in this Other. It reduces us to awe and places upon us a tremendous (and unbearable?) burden of responsibility. We become responsible for the death of the other.

It is as if that invisible death, ignored by the Other, whom already it concerns by the nakedness of its face, were already 'regarding' me prior to confronting me, and becoming the death that stares me in the face. The other man's death calls me into question, as if, by my possible indifference I had become the accomplice of the death to which the other, who cannot see it, is exposed; and it is as if, even before vowing myself to him, I had to answer for this death of the other, and to accompany the Other in his mortal solitude. The Other becomes my neighbour precisely through the way the face summons me, calls for me, begs for me, and in so doing, recalls my responsibility, and calls me into question.

(*ibid.*: 83)

This way, perhaps, madness lies. It is a very different way of relating with the Other, and surely is a dangerous way of encountering the Other. The weight of responsibility it engenders is heavy. It is certainly transgressive of a relation of binary opposition and hierarchical reference: A:NotA is hardly applicable to Levinas' approach to difference. The sense of Self is greatly diminished.

This is alterity. The term alterity has its etymological roots in the Latin *alterare*, alter, meaning other. Elizabeth Grosz defines it thus:

A form of otherness irreducible to and unable to be modelled on any form of projection of or identification with the subject. The term refers to a notion of the other outside the binary opposition between self and other, an independent and autonomous other with its own qualities and attributes. The other is outside of, unpredictable by and ontologically prior to the subject.

(Grosz 1990: xiv)

In this conception the Other is autonomous, independent of the subject, the One. An Other not constructed by reference to sameness, as prior to the subject, is alterity embodied. This conception can, I suggest, be read as expressing a desire for difference *as* difference. The fundamental differences between this conception of alterity and that of Otherness conceived of along binary terms are that, for Levinas, the other is autonomous; the other is prior to the subject or self. We have here an approach to the relation of Self and Other that is not dualistic, nor fragmentary, nor holistic. It is quite profoundly utopian, in the sense of that word used throughout this book. It attempts to foresee an unforeseeable relation of Self and Other, to inscribe onto our consciousness something entirely other to that ordained by our culture and traditions of philosophy. It is not, however, a cosy relation. It is not comfortable, familiar or intimate. Rather it is fraught with risks and dangers.

There is a feminist utopia in which a similar approach to the Other is attempted. It comes from a different intellectual tradition to that occupied by Levinas but is, nonetheless, reminiscent of both the awe and repulsion that he evokes. Monique Wittig describes her feminism as 'materialist lesbianism'. She is concerned to explore a non-dualistic constriction of gender which, she claims, can be found in lesbian subjectivity. Unlike heterosexual women, who are lined up with the construct of Woman, lesbian subjectivity is autonomously defined, without reference to Man or men. She characterises this as 'the lesbian position':

> lesbianism is the only concept I know of which is beyond the categories of sex (Woman and Man), because the designated subject (lesbian) is *not* a woman, economically, politically, or ideologically.
>
> (Wittig 1981: 20)

In the utopian fiction *The Lesbian Body* (1973), Wittig writes of the Other with awe and reverence. The entire book is an inscription of the lesbian body: the autonomous female body. In this book men have ceased to exist. It is about women that Wittig calls 'Amazons': 'The Amazons are women who live among themselves and for themselves at all the generally accepted levels: fictional, symbolic, actual' (*ibid.*, Author's note, p. 9). The text is broken into segments and each evokes a different scene. Every now and then this text is interspersed with pages of capitalised lists of female body parts, some anatomically correct, some imagined. She is, she says, writing the woman's body as has never before been written. Her concern with identity, explored in her theoretical texts, is expressed here through splitting the 'I' (*J/e*). This is shown in translation as 'I', 'm/e' and 'm/y'. She splits the personal pronoun in this way to express the sense of alienation – separation from 'self' – that she experiences as a woman, using masculine language. Her syntax is disrupted for the same reason.

> 'I' (*Je*) obliterates the fact that *elle* or *elles* are submerged in *il* or *ils*, i.e., that all feminine persons are complementary to the masculine persons. ... *J/e* is the symbol of the lived, rendering experience which is m/y writing, of this

cutting in tow which throughout literature is the exercise of a language which does not constitute m/e as subject. *J/e* poses the ideological and historic question of feminine subjects.

> (*ibid.*, Author's note, pp. 10–11)

The style of the book is poetic, and reads beautifully, even in translation. Here is the opening sentence:

> In this dark adored adorned gehenna say your farewells m/y very beautiful one m/y very strong one m/y very indomitable one m/y very learned one m/y very ferocious one m/y very gentle one m/y best beloved to what they, the women, call affection tenderness or gracious abandon.

> (Wittig 1973: 15)

The story is told in the first person, addressed to a lover. It is erotic and sensual. It is also startling, disturbing and violent. By the end of the first page, for instance, we find this:

> The gleam of your teeth your joy your sorrow the hidden life of your viscera your blood your arteries your veins your hollow habitations your organs your nerves their rupture their spurting for death slow decomposition stench being devoured by worms your open skull, all will be equally unbearable to her.

> (*ibid.*: 15)

The 'her' in this passage is another woman, the 'I' of the book will love her lover despite and because of all this putrefaction and decay. That love is at the heart of this book. At no point though is the Other – the lover – approached in a knowing, grasping acquisitive sense. I say this despite the existence of passages like this one:

> M/y most delectable one *I* set about eating you, m/y tongue moistens the helix of your ear delicately gliding around, m/y tongue inserts itself in the auricle, it touches the antihelix, m/y teeth seek the lobe, they begin to gnaw at it, m/y tongue gets into your ear canal.

> (*ibid.*: 24)

She proceeds to eat – but this is not a devouring of the strangeness of the Other. The Other is not consumed for her difference (Derrida), desired for her absence (Lacan) or reduced to sameness (Levinas). Rather she is, in this way, celebrated and adored. Wittig is attentive to the Other. Physically she is discovered and unravelled and known and loved. But there is no sense of property relation or hierarchy in this relation. It is disturbing, but not for its ontological claims. Throughout the book is a sense of awe at this unknowable Other.

Your very precise very soft voice reaches m/e sooner than *I* catch sight of you causing me to tremble with impatience ... while *I* am paralysed by the suddenness of your advent.   (*ibid.*: 25)

You look at m/e. M/y knees give way   (*ibid.*: 33)

I look at you m/y unique one.   (*ibid.*: 45)

You are face to face with m/e sphinx of clay.   (*ibid.*: 47)

Always though, a sense of strangeness is retained.

This is, I suggest, reminiscent of a Levinasian encounter with the Other for a number of reasons: it is awful – in both senses of that word. The Other overwhelms the author and supersedes her expectations and her knowledge. No attempt is made to grasp, though the body is recited in its minutiae parts. Awe does not permit this. The different kind of knowing appears to be desired here. It is loving. The Other is desired in its entirety but not possessed. It is awful also because it evokes a sense of neurosis, madness and obsession. It is a vertiginous love.

Letting go of the desire to possess the Other is a utopian and a transgressive approach to the world. It breaks with 'normal' and taken-for-granted patterns of behaviour. It creates a space in which the Other can be Other: different and strange without becoming a threat to us, to our integrity or our identity, because we do not need it to affirm our identity. However, in so doing, we place ourselves on unsafe and unknown terrain. The risks to sanity and security are implicit in Levinas and become particularly apparent in Wittig. She would say that it is worth the risk. The following comes from her earlier utopia, *Les Guerillères*:

If I take over the world, let it be to dispossess myself of it immediately, let it be to forge new links between myself and the world.

(Wittig 1971: 107)

'New' individualism: New Age conceptions of Self and Other

New Age accounts of the relationship of Self to Other are a curious hybrid of holism and individualism. This is underdeveloped in academic terms and I shall be drawing here mainly on the accounts of members of the Findhorn Community. I shall begin with a lengthy extract from one interview: that with Simon. Simon was, at the time of this visit, near completion of the Student Year Programme. His testimony is typical in terms of its content; all members of this community expressed similar beliefs and feelings. In this sense, although what follows is a very personal statement, it is also representative – or typical – of an experience of Findhorn. Simon is articulate and lucid and the passages below comprise a continuous narrative. I shall include the entire response to my question and not just the statements relevant to Self and Other. In this way I hope to convey a feel of the context of these statements.

LS: What first attracted you to this community?

Simon: I can remember very clearly, I arrived for Experience Week. I knew about this place from when I was 7 years old and it took me 20 years to get here and I came because of a sense of desperation really with what was going on in my life back home. . . . I needed to find a way out from my environment and a relationship had broken down and I was very unhappy. I arrived here in a real state but quite excited about finally coming to Findhorn and see what it was all about. I can remember the day I arrived here I felt quite sick, physically and . . . I was very low and I walked into Cluny to arrange the Experience Week on the Saturday morning – and suddenly I just felt very at home.

This is an oft-repeated phrase and it has resonance with my own experience of visiting Cluny. A sense of 'coming home' or 'belonging' is common amongst first- or second-time visitors.

Simon: People took an interest in me. I felt listened to. I felt cared for without being smothered. I mean, I felt like it was my responsibility, everything was within my responsibility, you know, I wasn't having my power taken away from me and yet I felt nurtured and cared for too which was like a fine line for me, you know. And as the week went on I first of all had this very strong sense of belonging within the group and just an openness to something. I felt very safe.

Again, this is familiar and is a common experience of the introductory programme: Findhorn Experience Week. The feeling of security, and being in a safe place are apparent amongst visitors. There is also here a reference to one of the paradoxes of the Findhorn approach to responsibility. People are encouraged to be their best and most true Self at the Foundation. They receive support and nurturence from each other and from members. But responsibility lies with the individual. Self and Other are in a relationship of process, but the ownership of the outcome is with the individual: the Self. Simon accounts for this in terms of retaining his 'power': his sovereignty of Self.

    Those who are responsive to the interpersonal environment feel able to take risks with themselves, to let go of former behaviour patterns of defensiveness and to 'open': both to their 'higher Self' and to that Self in others.

Simon: For me this was a space where I could really open up and show myself and not be judged. I could be listened to, mostly, not to be judged but just to be accepted for who I was and then – what was really incredible – was having people who were open enough to really (and it didn't feel fake, you know) but actually just to say what they thought about me. They said some very very positive things and it really ... I just realised how important it is to be able to tell people what you think of them, in a positive way. I wasn't used to it and at first it was uncomfortable for me to have, you know, nice things said about me. Then I realised actually it was me that was judging myself, because I was having difficulties accepting these things, so the week was very much about: 'Gosh, maybe I'm ok, maybe I'm quite a nice person. Maybe I'm not so awful'. Once I started to focus on that side and to look at the positive in myself (Eileen always says, you can open doors with a look ... you look to the positive to see the divine in each other and I guess that starts by seeing the divine in ourselves and seeing the very best in ourselves) I think that began a kind of process for me of really, a path of really beginning to do that for myself. To change my perception of myself; to realise that I have a right to be in this world, I haven't done anything wrong, I don't need forgiveness for anything, that basically I'm a good person – and that sounds really obvious – but I think, how many of us go around not believing that? So it was very affirming and so were the love that I experienced and the openness and the honesty from people.

The community has few rules – but two important ones are stressed at the first meeting of Experience Week. The first is that no illegal drugs are permitted on the premises. The second is that people should speak in 'I statements'. For instance, to say 'you know how it's really irritating when people interrupt you ...' is considered an evasion of responsibility. To speak in the first person singular: to use only I statements is to 'own' one's feelings and to accept responsibility for them. Instead, the speaker is encouraged to ask permission to 'share' with the other person whatever it is that they have to say. 'Lucy, may I share something with you?' Assuming acquiescence, the thing is then shared. Some have trouble sharing positive things that they feel about each other; others find it hard to express negative reactions. All are given equal space and seen as of import. Simon's account shows how startling it can be to receive positive affirmations about one's self. Those who respond well to this way of communicating find this liberating and self-affirming. Articulating and owning one's own emotional response is seen as a route towards the best of one's Self. I shall return on p. 149 to the reference in parentheses and the spiritual dimension of the Findhorn approach to Self below. First though, Simon's testimony as to his first week concludes thus:

Simon: By the end of the week I was in a very good state. I released a lot. I found this place where I could release a lot of emotions that I'd been holding on to and I was able to experience some intimacy in the group, which was something which I felt I hadn't allowed into my life when I was living in London. I'd lost that intimacy, that connection with other human beings. I had it with, like, one or two close friends but even then it was difficult to sustain it because our lifestyles were very, you know, using a diary to arrange to meet somebody for, you know, even a best friend to go for a drink. And intimacy for me is difficult ... and I came here and I found that every moment of the day was an opportunity for intimacy ... you know, whether you're having a cup of tea with someone or doing your laundry or whatever – this was a 24 hour a day, 7 days a week place.

It is stressed at the first meeting that Findhorn is not a therapy centre, but rather a spiritual community in which the Self can be explored. They claim to provide the context: the space, in which this can be tried. (In this sense it is a utopian space.) It is not a psychotherapy unit or a counselling encounter. The outcome described by Simon might have come from professional therapy, but that is not what the Findhorn Foundation affords.

The spiritual practice at Findhorn is eclectic and varies amongst individuals, as do personal beliefs. It is though a New Age community, and is influential within this body of thought. Certain core values are expressed. One has been mentioned already, and this concerns the ownership of responsibility. Another is the belief that within one's self is something transcendent. This is variously described as 'God', 'divinity', 'spirit' and other referential terms that imply a 'higher' being. This, it is believed, can be manifested in the Self. We have access to 'God' – through the Self, where he/she/it resides. The process of contacting this Self is called 'attunement'. People give varying accounts of the ways in which they attune to spirit, for some it is through work (discussed in the previous chapter), for others it is accessed through 'inner listening': meditation, prayer or fasting. Yet others find divinity in nature.

The 'opening' referred to at Findhorn is reminiscent of Arne Naess's route to Self-Realisation, and Warwick Fox is a figure named by some as a personal inspiration. Self-transformation is certainly fundamental to the Findhorn Foundation's self-rationale:

> It is the transformation of this everyday self [our personality] into the Self within which provides the challenge of the new spirituality.
>
> (Riddell 1996: 41)

> Only as you expand your consciousness, are you open and receptive to the new all around you and can be attuned to new thoughts, new ideas, new ways of life.
>
> (Caddy 1994: 102)

The tone and vocabulary of New Age literature is quite alienating. In terms of content, the process of the desired transformation is similar to that of the deep ecology. It is an 'opening': an extension of awareness. It is, however, both more and less Self-referential than is deep ecology. The stress in the New Age approach to Self is on receptivity. One opens – permits – gives access to the 'divine' within. This is not unproblematic. To claim divinity as one's source is surely dangerous. It is to claim unassailable access to the truth. Conversational claims that 'God spoke to me' are not uncommon. Eileen Caddy, erstwhile spiritual 'leader' of the community, is said to have received regular 'channelling' – or communication from God. Others claim it too, with what is sometimes a surprising familiarity:

> Channelling, the ability to receive inner guidance, has been much mystified and romanticised but it is an easily learned technique, available with a little training to all who turn inwards for translating God's energy, always there, into communication.
>
> (Riddell 1996: 40)

This model of Self is receptive to the Other. In one sense, Otherness (as spirit, God, nature) is greeted as an accessible familiar. This is the 'god within'. God (spirit, nature) becomes part of the Self, or *vice versa*. The gardeners at Findhorn often talk of connection with and respect for the spirit of the plants with which they work. Here the affinity with deep ecology is apparent. A receptive model of Self might be (paradigmatically?) different to the encompassing, consuming or acquisitive Self. The Other is not automatically negated or appropriated by this approach. Other people and beings are given space to 'grow' and self-improve, and responsibility is for the Self alone. Only in these conditions can sanity and intimacy co-exist, it is suggested. This can be (and is at Findhorn) described as allowing respect and space for the Other.

There is a tension here though. The Findhorn approach could equally be described in terms of Self-centred individualism, or pure selfishness. It surely has roots in classical liberal thought such as that of John Locke. Locke's theory of property was introduced in the previous chapter. Briefly though, here the individual is sovereign by virtue of self-ownership. Here, each individual has original possession of his/her own person and an 'appropriate' responsibility for Self. The Self has, in itself, an original God-given right to property. Drawing on the Christian tradition, Locke states that God gave to man his autonomy and the world: 'nature' is at man's disposal. Even in a state that pre-dates civil society and government, says Locke, man has self-possession. By extension he owns his labour and that with which he mingles his labour. This is how Locke accounts for the right to own external possessions. We are, in this state, he says, in competition with others for scarce provisions and goods (things that we desire). So long as we are not wasteful, we have right of first possession. This takes us straight back into an oppositional paradigm.

In one sense, the Findhorn Self is profoundly irresponsible for others, in another it owns deep responsibility for self. But the individualism of the New Age is, I suggest, inherited from the older tradition, as is the attitude towards property and wealth. 'Poverty consciousness' is held to be at least partly responsible for economic inequality. An inversion of the positive affirmation, poverty consciousness can make you attract poverty and deprivation. This view is surely dangerous in political terms. Accountability and responsibility cannot belong solely with Self – enlightened though it may be. Wider external factors cannot, surely, be willed away.

Conclusions

Consideration of Self/Other relations touches upon the following issues:

- Relationships. What guides and grounds our relationships with other individuals, groups and species? What accounts do we offer ourselves to explain and justify these relations? What are the implications of the accounts?
- Responsibility. To what extent are we responsible for ourselves and for others and why?
- Identity. How is our sense of identity in relation to others formed?

The answers provided by the dualistic model of Self are restricting, slippery and dangerous. Self and Other are dissimilar. Difference is to be feared and quashed. Self and Other are in perpetual opposition. Evading this paradigm is difficult. It seeps insidiously into the work of the psychoanalytic theorists. It is at the heart of social psychology. Holistic approaches and that of the New Age appear to avoid it only by assertion of some divine rightness. Approaches that insist on retaining Self and Other, but which envisage a different mediating paradigm are the most rigorous. Even here, though, the old dualisms slip in. I opened my discussion of Levinas by stating that he does not attempt closure: 'utopia' I said 'as a vision of Otherness, remains uninscribed – almost'. I argued that Levinas' approach to death is utopian in this sense. His work *Time and the Other* gestures towards several other utopias of Otherness (or spaces of alterity). These are femininity, the erotic relationship and paternity. In each of these instances, he is prescriptive, referring to accepted and conventional terms of reference. Femininity, to take just one example, is described as dark, moist and modest (Levinas in Hand 1989: 50). The associations are traditional and the utopia is drawn from a dualistic paradigm.[3] Even Levinas falls back onto dualistic ground.

   Each of the approaches considered here is problematic in some way. From the encounter though has come the following:

From the holistic view:

- radical egalitarianism;
- empathy;
- a stress of interconnectedness.

3 Credit here is due to colleagues in the reading group at the School of Politics at Nottingham.

From the heterogeneous view:

- a reconceptualisation of the significance of difference;
- awe;
- an approach to the world that does not seek fully to comprehend it.

From the New Age community at Findhorn:

- frustration;
- inspiration.

The lived reality of Self and Other at Findhorn communities is complex and intellectually frustrating. It is a curious hybrid of high liberalism (combining theories of self-ownership, radical individualism regarding responsibility and poverty) with deep ecology (whence the melting of boundaries of Self and Other). An approach that desires more space for incommensurate difference is, I think, less likely to lead to appropriate relations than is one that seeks to embrace and comprehend the Other. It might be that the Findhorn approach permits this, albeit problematic in intellectual terms. A neoliberal–postmodern–ecologist Self? This is surely eclecticism at its worst. However, elements of all of these traditions inform the New Age self and – well, it does seem to work. Even the briefest visit to the community at Findhorn affords a glimpse of a place in which people are in a process that seeks peace with Self and Others.

There are, it seems, no easy answers to the questions that are provoked by a study of Self and Other relations. The use of utopian bodies of thought and people as vehicles for exploration has, however, yielded something of value. It is possible that we may have to give up both the quest for understanding the other and the privilege of difference.

Difference, if approached as incommensurable, is not a hurdle to overcome. We might need to address the incommesurably different Other and for this a common vocabulary will be required – one that does not 'continue to speak this sameness' (Irigaray 1980: 67). Politics would then become a matter of negotiation and coalition in which identities are permitted to be strategic, shifting and multiple. Greater openness to the Other might, in this utopia, issue a relation that permits the Other. This would be an approach that does not seek to possess.

Conclusion
Utopian Bodies

How can I touch you, when you are not there?

(Luce Irigaray 1980: 67)

Interesting things happen when bodies meet: we look, think, feel, touch, and/ or communicate. The meeting of bodies produces change in those bodies: rarely do they leave one another unaffected by the encounter. Often this is unpredictable and contingent. This book has endeavoured to contrive an introduction of bodies of thought and people and has initiated a process of dialogue and exchange. Ideas, insights and inspiration have flowed between these bodies and the result is a prodigal child with an uncertain future.

The debates in the chapters above exceed the parameters of the bodies consulted. A plurality of voices pertaining to feminism, deep ecology, the utopian canon and deconstructive theory have been focused to speak (at times simultaneously) to a number of complex theoretical concepts that have contemporary political relevance. The result (and process) has not, hopefully, been dissonant. Rather, resonant chords have reflected from one body to another as new ground is cleared for debate. This is one function of the transgressive form of utopianism advocated here. It will frustrate the desires of those who long for complete answers or solutions to the dilemmas raised. There is no utopia of perfection here. There is only space for further exploration.

However, the themes of these chapters *can* be connected in a more or less coherent fashion to offer an account of one direction that might afford a sustainable critique and alternative. The chapters combine to articulate an account of the ways in which the public, the private and the political have been studied to the detriment of the body. This impacts on bodies of thought and bodies of people and comprises a restrictive worldview. Connected to this is a particular approach to property that informs the ways in which we relate to one another.

All of the approaches consulted in Chapter 5 aim, more or less successfully, to move us away from the liberal theory of ownership, property and the law that was considered in Chapter 4. Here the sovereign individual is possessed of self-ownership. The Self is the individual's property. Ownership of self is sanctioned in law, and this gives us rights against others. This is founded in a certain approach to ownership and rights. Ownership (sanctioned in law) affords rights.

These rights are held in opposition to the will and agency of others. This speaks to the oppositional construction of relations of Self to Other.

Much of the terrain covered in these debates includes the language of the private sphere. I began with John Locke's theory of property, which takes as its starting point the body and its labours. The work of a self-owning being results in rightful ownership of external possessions. Prior to this act of human labour though we are, for Locke, the property of God. God made us and has therefore rights of property over us. Even in the State of Nature, for instance, Locke permits no space for self-harm. Surely the self-owning individual has autonomy over the disposal of his person? Locke says not:

> For men being all the Workmanship of one Omnipotent, and infinitely wise Maker; All the Servants of one Sovereign Master, sent into the World by his order and about his business, they are his Property, whose Workmanship they are, made to last during his, not another's pleasure.
>
> (Locke, *Two Treatises*, Bk. II, Section 8)

The irony of this position should not escape us. His approach (and that of subsequent liberal thought) is profoundly and unabashedly rationalistic. Reason is the king of the castle that is the Lockean body. Desire, emotion and irrationalism are all the property of the non-political private sphere. In Chapter 3, I introduced some insights from feminist thought on this and attempted a disruption of the easy association of the political with the public. The body itself has long been the property of the private sphere. Bodies excrete. Bodies are sensual. The body is the site of voluptuousness, pain and defiance of will. Bodies have babies. Bodies shit and sweat and smell. What place for this mass of matter in high theory? For Locke, the body is the original site of human property, albeit a second-hand gift from a disembodied God. Bodies think and act and speak and are political agents, citizens and lovers.

My point is not that the body has previously had no role in political thought, but rather that this role has been implicit and neglected. I argued in Chapter 3 that the site of the political is a shifting one, that the public and the private are connected by observably porous boundaries. I suggested that attention to this might enable a more reflective and responsive approach to the world. The way that we study the world has an impact on that world. Methodology is not just an issue for pedants. This book seeks an approach that is appropriate to diversity and complexity but does not plunge into the abyss of cerebral incomprehensibility.

This approach is (perhaps) best facilitated in utopic spaces. Sorties into utopian spaces facilitate thought, speculation and creation. They are spaces free from constraint, limited only by imagination. They are places in which it is possible to conceive of − and then perhaps demand − the impossible (Moylan 1986). Transgression: deliberately stepping over accepted boundaries − is an intentional act of will. It aims at the creation of something other than the known and familiar.

It is not safe. It is not a route to stability. But it is, perhaps, safer in the protected confines of a utopian body.

Textual utopias create mental space that permits an estranged viewpoint to exist. The content of the viewpoint may not be palatable but we can, in these no-places, have a good look at it. Looking at intentional communities takes this a step further. They are contained communities in which it is possible to see utopias of, say communal ownership, in operation. However, attention to one facet of communal life gives a skewed picture. Always, alongside the idealistic is the practical. Communal ownership is a fine concept and has much merit ideologically. It is compatible with green, socialist and feminist utopias. Also it has very difficult aspects, which come often from the private sphere of relationships and domesticity and human relations. Intentional communities are living experiments as well as 'showcases' for an alternative way of life.

The centre can learn from the margins and the bodies consulted here are indeed marginal to the mainstream of political thought and everyday politics. Feminism is marginal in political authority and power. The ecological communities are marginal in cultural terms. Deep ecology and deconstruction are alienating and alienated by their radicalism and inaccessibility. However, these bodies offer inspiration and energy and a refreshing creativity. Also, they speak to the necessity of finding a new way forward. Whether or not these bodies comprise a bloc of opposition in practical terms, they do combine to articulate this need. Without radical deep-rooted change in the way that we think, they insist, things cannot change:

> How can I touch you, when you are not there?
> If we continue to speak this sameness, if we speak to each other as men
> have spoken for centuries, as they taught us to speak, we will fail each
> other. . . . Words will pass through our bodies, above our heads, and
> disappear, make us disappear.
>
> (Irigaray 1980: 67)

Bibliography

Alexander, P. and Gill, R. (eds) (1984) *Utopias*, London: Duckworth.

Anderson, V. (1991) *Alternative Economic Indicators*, London: Routledge.

Beilhartz, P. (1992) *Labour's Utopias*, London: Routledge.

Bahro, R. (1994) *Avoiding Social and Political Disaster: The Politics of World Transformation*, trans. P. Jenkins, Bath: Gateway Books.

Bammer, A. (1991) *Partial Visions: Feminism and Utopianism in the 1970s*, London: Routledge.

Barr, M. S. (ed.) (1981) *Future Females: A Critical Anthology*, Cincinnati: Bowling Green State University Press.

Barry, J. (1994) 'The limits of the shallow and the deep: Green politics, philosophy, and praxis', *Environmental Politics* 3, 369–94.

Barry, J. (1999) *Rethinking Green Politics*, London: Routledge.

Baudrillard, J. (1993) *The Transparency of Evil*, London: Pluto.

Biehl, J. (1991) *Rethinking Ecofeminist Politics*, Boston: South End Books.

Biehl, J. (1993) 'Problems in ecofeminism', *Society and Nature* 2(1).

Bloch, E. (1986) *The Principle of Hope*, 3 vols, Oxford: Blackwell.

Bookchin, M. (1980) *Towards an Ecological Society*, Montreal: Black Rose.

Braidotti, R. (1991) *Patterns of Dissonance*, Cambridge: Polity.

Brown, S. (1980) *Political Subjectivity*, New Haven: Yale University Press.

Bryson, V. (1992) *Feminist Political Theory*, Basingstoke: Macmillan.

Buckley, J. (1989) *Women and Identity in the Soviet Union*, London: Harvester Wheatsheaf.

Butler, J. and Scott, J. (1997) *Feminists Theorise the Political*, London: Routledge.

Caddy, E. (1994) *The Spirit of Findhorn*, Forres: Findhorn Press.

Cahoone, L. (ed.) (1996) *From Modernism to Postmodernism: An Anthology*, Oxford: Blackwell.

Callenbach, E. (1975) *Ecotopia*, Berkeley, CA: Banyon Books.

Carter, A. (1982) *The Passion of a New Eve*, London: Virago.

Caute, D. (1967) *Essential Writings of Karl Marx*, London: Panther.

Centre for Alternative Technology (CAT) 'Composting sewage' instruction leaflet.

Cixous, H. and Clement, C. (1986) *The Newly Born Woman*, trans. Betsy Wing, Brighton: Harvester Wheatsheaf.

Coates, C., How, J., Jones, L., Morris, W. and Wood, A. (eds) (1996/7) *Diggers and Dreamers: The Guide to Co-operative Living*, Winslow: D&D.

Collins, P. H. (1991) *Black Feminist Thought*, London: Routledge.

Conference proceedings (1997) *Eco-Villages and Sustainable Communities*, Forres: The Findhorn Press.

Coult, T. and Kershaw, B. (1995) *Engineers of the Imagination: The Welfare State Handbook*, London: Methuen.

Culler, J. (1987) *Deconstruction: Theory and Criticism after Structuralism*, London: Routledge.

Daly, M. (1979) *Gyn/Ecology: The Metaethics of Radical Feminism*, London: The Women's Press, 1987 edition.

Davies, J. C. (1981) 'The history of utopia: The chronology of nowhere' in Alexander and Gill (eds) *Utopia and the Ideal Society*, Cambridge: Cambridge University Press.

Derrida, J. (1972) 'Difference from margins of philosophy' in P. Kamuf (ed.) *A Derrida Reader: Between the Blinds*, Hemel Hempstead: Harvester Wheatsheaf.

Derrida, J. (1977) *Of Grammatology*, London/Baltimore: John Hopkins University Press.

Derrida, J. (1978) *Writing and Difference*, trans. Alan Bell, London: Routledge, 1995 edition.

Derrida, J. (1982) 'Choreographies in P. Kamuf (ed.) *A Derrida Reader: Between the Blinds*, Hemel Hempstead: Harvester Wheatsheaf.

Derrida, J. (1985) 'Des tours de Babel' in P. Kamuf (ed.) *A Derrida Reader: Between the Blinds*, Hemel Hempstead: Harvester Wheatsheaf.

Derrida, J. (1994) *Specters of Marx*, New York: Routledge.

Dickerson, D. (1997) *Property, Women and Politics*, Cambridge: Polity.

Dobson, A. (1990) *The Green Reader*, London: Andre Deutsch.

Dobson, A. (1995) *The Green Reader*, London: Routledge.

Eckersley, R. (1992) *Environmentalism and Political Theory*, London: UCL.

Ekins, P. (ed.) (1986) *The Living Economy*, London: Routledge and Kegan Paul.

Elshtain, J.B. (1981) *Public Man, Private Woman*, Oxford: Robertson.

Firestone, S. (1971) *The Dialectic of Sex*, London: Cape.

Flanagan, P. (ed.) (1979) *Theories of Property; Aristotle to Present*, Ontario: Wilfred University Press.

Foddy, W. (1994) *Constructing Interview Questions: Theory and Practice in Social Research*, Cambridge: Cambridge University Press.

Fourier, C. (1901) *Design for Utopia: Selected Writings*, New York: Schocken Books.

Fox, W. (1990) *Towards a Transpersonal Ecology: Developing the Foundations for Environmentalism*, London and Boston: Shambhala.

Freidan, B. (1981) *The Second Stage*, London: Michael Joseph.

Freud, S. (1931) 'Female sexuality' See Freud (1977).

Freud, S. (1977) *On Sexuality*, Penguin: Middlesex.

Garner, R. (1996) *Environmental Politics*, Hemel Hempstead: Harvester.

Garry, A. and Pearsall, M. (eds) (1989) *Women, Knowledge and Reality*, London: Unwin.

Geoghegan, V. (1987) *Utopianism and Marxism*, London: Methuen.

Goodwin, B. (1978) *Social Science and Utopia*, Brighton: Harvester.

Griffin, S. (1989) 'Split culture' in J. Plant (ed.) *Healing the Wounds: The Promise of Ecofeminism*, London: Merlin Press.

Grosz, E (1990a) *Jacques Lacan*, Routledge: London.

Grosz, E (1990b) 'A Note on Essentialism and Difference' in S. Gunew (ed.) *Feminist Knowledge: Critique and Construct*, London: Routledge.

Grunnebaum, J. (1987) *Private Ownership*, London: Routledge.

Gunew, S. (1990) *Feminist Knowledge: Critique and Construct*, London: Routledge.

Hammersley, M. (1995) *The Politics of Social Research*, London: Sage.

Hand, S. (1989) *The Levinas Reader*, Oxford: Blackwell, 1994 edition.

Hirschmann, N. J. and Stefano, C. (1996) *Revisioning the Political*, Oxford: Westview Press.

Hobbes, T. (1968) *Leviathan*, London: Penguin.

Hollowell, P. (1982) 'On the operationalisation of property' in P. Hollowell (ed.) *Property and Social Relations*, London: Heinemann.

Hollowell, P. (ed.) (1982) *Property and Social Relations*, London: Heinemann.

Holstein, J. (1995) *The Active Interview*, Thousand Oaks: Sage.

hooks, b. (1984) *From Margin to Centre*, London: Pluto.

Humphrey, M. (1999) 'Ontological determinism' in J. Katz, M. Light and D. Rothenberg (eds) *Beneath the Surface*, Cambridge, Mass.: MIT Press.

Irigaray, L. (1990) 'When our lips speak together', *Signs* 6(1).

Jagger, A. (1983) *Feminist Politics and Human Nature*, Brighton: Harvester.

Jagger, A. (1989) 'Love and knowledge: Emotion in feminist epistemology' in A. Garry and M. Pearsall (eds) *Women, Knowledge and Reality*, London: Unwin.

Jagger, A. and Bordo, S. (1992) *Gender/Body/Knowledge*, New Brunswick: Rutgers University Press.

Jorgenson, D. L. (1989) *Participant Observation: A Methodology for Human Societies*, Newbury Park: Sage.

Kamuf, P. (1991) (ed.) *A Derrida Reader: Between the Blinds*, Hemel Hempstead: Harvester Wheatsheaf.

Kemp, P. and Wall, D. (1990) *A Green Manifesto for the 1990s*, London: Penguin.

Kemp, S. and Squires, J. (1997) *Feminisms*, Oxford: Oxford University Press.

Knowles, D. (1963) *Monastic Order in England*, vol. II, *Institutional*, Cambridge: Cambridge University Press.

Kourany, J. A., Sterba, J. P. and Tong, R. (eds) (1993) *Feminist Philosophies: Problems, Theories and Applications*, Hemel Hempstead: Harvester Wheatsheaf.

Kumar, K. (1991) *Utopianism*, Buckingham: Oxford University Press.

Lacan, J. (1977) 'The signification of the phallus', in *Ecits: A Selection*, London: Tavistock, 1977 (first published in 1958).

Laslett, P. (1964) *Locke's Two Treatises of Government*, Cambridge: Cambridge University Press.

Leopold, A. (1949) *A Sand Country Almanac*, reproduced in Dobson (1990).

Levi, P. (1979) *If This Is A Man*, London: Abacus, 1998 edition.

Levinas, E. (1969) *Totality and Infinity*, trans. A. Lingis, Pittsburgh: Duquesne University Press, 1995 edition.

Levinas, E. (1987) *Time and the Other*, trans. R. Cohen, Pittsburgh: Duquesne University Press.

Levinas, E. (1989) *The Levinas Reader*, S. Hand (ed.), Oxford: Blackwell.

Levitas, R. (1990) *The Concept of Utopia*, Hemel Hempstead: Philip Allan.

Lloyd, G. (1989) 'The man of reason', in A. Garry and M. Pearsall (eds) *Women, Knowledge and Reality*, London: Unwin.

Locke, J. (1689) See Laslett (1964).

Marsh, D. and Stoker, G. (1995) *Theory and Methods in Political Science*, Basingstoke: Macmillan.

Marx, K. and Engels, F. (1969) *Manifesto of the Communist Party* 1888, Moscow: Progress.

Marx, K. (1844/6) *Economic and Philosophical Manuscripts of 1844*, in Caute (1961).
Marx, K. (1961) *Capital* (vol. I) 1867, London: Lawrence and Wishart.
Marx, K. (1963) *The German Ideology* 1846, London: Lawrence and Wishart.
Mathews, F. (1991) *The Ecological Self*, London: Routledge.
McCracken, D. G. (1988) *The Long Interview*, London: Sage.
McDowell, L. and Pringle, R. (1992) *Defining Women*, Cambridge: Polity.
McKay, G. (1996) *Senseless Acts of Beauty*, London: Verso.
Macpherson, C. B. (1978) *Property: Mainstream and Critical Positions*, Oxford: Black-well.
Mead, G. H. (1934) *Mind, Self, and Society*, Chicago: Chicago University Press.
Mellor, M. (1992) 'Green politics: Ecofeminist, ecofeminine, or ecomasculine? *Environmental Politics* 1(2).
Merchant, C. (1990) *The Death of Nature*, New York: Harper.
Metzger, D. (1989) 'Invoking the grove', in J. Plant (ed.) *Healing the Wounds: The Promise of Ecofeminism*, London: Merlin Press.
Mitchell, J. and Rose, J. (1982) *Feminine Sexuality*, London: Macmillan, 1987 edition.
More, T. (1965) *The Complete Works of Thomas More*, vol. IV, *Utopia*, New Haven and London: Yale University Press.
Morris, W. (1993) *News for Nowhere*, London, Routledge (first published in 1890).
Morton, A. L. (1952) *The English Utopia*, London: Lawrence and Wishart.
Moylan, T. (1986) *Demand the Impossible: Science Fiction and the Utopian Imagination*, London: Methuen.
Naess, A. (1973) 'The shallow and the deep: Long-range ecology movement', *Inquiry* 16.
Naess, A. (1989) *Ecology, Community, and Lifestyle: Outline of an Ecosophy*, trans. D. Rothenberg, Cambridge: Cambridge University Press.
Nicholson, L. (ed.) (1990) *Feminism/Postmodernism*, London: Routledge.
O'Riordan, T. (1976) *Environmentalism*, London: Pion.
Pateman, C. (1988) *The Sexual Contract*, Cambridge: Polity.
Pearson, C. (1981) 'Coming home: Four feminist utopias and patriarchal experi-ence', in M. S. Barr (ed.) *Future Females: A Critical Anthology*, Cincinnati: Bowling Green State University Press.
Pepper, D. (1989) *The Roots of Modern Environmentalism*, London: Routledge.
Pepper, D. (1991) *Communes and the Green Vision*, London: Green Print.
Phillips, A. and Barrett, M. (1996) *Destabilising Theory*, Cambridge: Polity.
Piercy, M. (1979) *Woman on the Edge of Time*, London: The Women's Press, 1987 edition.
Pierson, C. (1995) *Socialism after Communism: the new market socialism*, Cambridge: Polity.
Pierson, C. (1998) *Beyond the Welfare State*, Cambridge: Polity, second edition.
Plant, J. (ed.) (1989) *Healing the Wounds: The Promise of Ecofeminism*, London: Merlin Press.
Plato (1969) *The Republic*, London: Penguin.
Plumwood, V. (1993a) 'Feminism and ecofeminism', *Society and Nature* 2(1).
Plumwood, V. (1993b) *Feminism and the Mastery of Nature*, London: Routledge.
Porritt, J. (1984) *Seeing Green*, Oxford: Basil Blackwell.
Rainbow Tribe Leaflet 'A short guide to the Rainbow Co-operative Communities Project'.
Reeve, A. (1986) *Property*, London: Macmillan.

Regan, T. (1988) *The Case for Animal Rights*, London: Routledge.

Richardson, D. and Robinson, V. (eds) (1993) *Introducing Women's Studies*, Basingstoke: Macmillan.

Riddell, C. (1996) *The Findhorn Community*, Forres: Findhorn Press.

Rosser, S. P. (1993) 'Re-visioning clinical research: Gender and the ethics of experimental design', in J. A. Kourany, J. P. Sterba and R. Tong (eds) *Feminist Philosophies: Problems, Theory and Applications*, Hemel Hempstead: Harvester Wheatsheaf.

Rousseau, J.-J. (1988) *The Social Contract*, London: Penguin.

Ryan, A. (1987) *Property*, Milton Keynes: Open University Press.

Sale, K. (1985) *Dwellers in the Land: The Bioregional Vision*, San Francisco: Sierra Club.

Salleh, A. (1997) *Ecofeminism as Politics*, London: Zed Books.

Sargent, L. T. (1994) 'The three faces of utopianism revisited', in *Utopian Studies* 15(1).

Sargisson, L. (1996) *Contemporary Feminist Utopianism*, London: Routledge.

Schumacher, F. (1974) *Small is Beautiful*, London: Abacus.

Seel, B. (1997a) 'Strategies of resistance of the Pollock Free State Road Protest Camp', unpublished PhD thesis.

Seel, B. (1997b) 'The Findhorn Community' from 'Strategic identities: Strategy, culture, and consciousness in the Road Protest and New Age', unpublished PhD thesis.

Shanley, M. L and Pateman, C. (eds) (1991) *Feminist Interpretations and Political Theory*, Cambridge: Polity.

Sichtermann, B. (1986) *Femininity: The Politics of the Personal*, trans. J. Whitlam, Cambridge: Polity.

Simmons, I. G. (1993) *Interpreting Nature: Cultural Constructions of the Environment*, London: Routledge.

Smith, J. A., Harre, R. and Van Langenhowe, L. (eds) (1995) *Rethinking Methods in Psychology*, London, Thousand Oaks: Sage.

Spretnak, C. (1989) 'Towards an ecofeminist spirituality', in J. Plant (ed.) *Healing the Wounds: The Promise of Ecofeminism*, London: Merlin Press.

Still, J. (1997) *Feminine Economies*, Manchester: Manchester University Press.

Talbott, J. (1997) *Simply Build Green*, Forres: Findhorn Press.

The Findhorn Foundation (1999) *Core Programmes*.

'Trees for Life Newsletter', *Caledonia Wild!* Summer, 1997.

Tronto, J. C. (1996) 'Care as a political concept', in N. J. Hirschmann and C. Stefano (eds) *Revisioning the Political*, Oxford: Westview Press.

Van Parjis, P. (1995) *Real Freedom for All: What, If Anything, Can Justify Capitalism?*, Oxford: Clarendon.

Waldron, J. (1988) *The Right to Private Property*, Oxford: Clarendon.

Wall, D. (1990) *A Green Manifesto for the 1990s*, London: Penguin.

Wittig, M. (1971) *Les Guerillères*, trans. D. Le Vay, London: David Owen.

Wittig, M. (1973) *The Lesbian Body*, trans. R. Owen, Boston: Beacon Press.

Wittig, M. (1981) 'One is not born a woman', in Wittig (1992).

Wittig, M. (1992) *The Straight Mind and Other Essays*, Hemel Hempstead: Harvester.

Witz, A. (1993) 'Women and work', in D. Richardson and V. Robinson (eds) *Introducing Women's Studies*, Basingstoke: Macmillan.

Young, I. M. (1986) 'Impartiality and the civic public: Some implications of feminist critics of modern political theory', *Praxis International* 5(4).

Young, I. M. (1990) 'The ideal of community and the politics of difference', in L. Nicholson (ed.) *Feminism/Postmodernism*, London: Routledge.

Young, S. (1993) *The Politics of the Environment*, Manchester: Baseline Books.

Appendix A

Fully Mutual Rules of the Blackcurrant Housing Co-operative Limited registered under the Industrial and Provident Societies Act 1965. Model FM10. Register No. 26307. 12 October 1988.

Name, objects, registered office

1 The name of the Association shall be Blackcurrant Housing Co-operative Limited (in these rules referred to as the Co-operative).

2 The objects of the Co-operative shall be:

 a The construction, conversion, improvement and management on the co-operative principle of dwellings for occupation by members of the Co-operative under an agreement to occupy them (hereinafter referred to as the Agreement) granted to them by the Co-operative.

 b The provision and improvement on the co-operative principle of land or buildings for purposes connected with the requirements of the members occupying the houses provided or managed by the Co-operative.

3 The Co-operative shall have power to do all things necessary or expedient for the fulfilment of its objects.

4 The Co-operative shall not trade for profit.

5 The Registered Office of the Co-operative shall be at:

24 St Michael's Avenue
Abington
Northampton
NN1 4JN

Share capital

6 a The share capital of the Co-operative shall consist of shares of the nominal value of One Pound each issued to the members of the Co-operative upon admission to membership.

 b Shares shall be neither withdrawable nor transferable, shall carry no right to interest, dividend or bonus and shall be forfeited and cancelled on cessation of membership from whatever cause and the amount paid thereon shall become the property of the Membership.

7 a The members of the Co-operative shall be persons whose names are entered on the register of members (the Share register).

  b Only tenants and prospective tenants are eligible to become members.

  c Prospective tenants shall be those persons whose names are entered in a register of prospective tenants, which shall be kept by the Co-operative.

  d A member shall hold one share only in the Co-operative.

8 a Application for membership shall be considered under the procedure laid down by the general meeting.

  b A final decision on the acceptance of applicants for membership shall be taken by the general meeting.

If the application is approved, the Co-operative will issue the applicant with one share upon payment of One Pound.

9 a A member shall cease to be a member if he or she:

    i dies, or

    ii is expelled by a general meeting in accordance with subsection (b) of this rule, or

    iii resigns in person at a meeting or in writing to the Secretary prior to a meeting, or has his or her agreement terminated, in which case he or she shall cease to be a member seven days after the agreement comes to an end, unless by that time he or she has entered into a new Agreement with the association, or

    iv ceases to occupy the housing provided by the Association, or

    v is a prospective tenant, and has notified the Association in writing that he or she no longer requires accommodation, in which case his or her name shall be removed from the register of prospective tenants.

  b i A member may be expelled by a resolution carried by the votes of three-quarters of the members present in person and voting at a general meeting of the Co-operative of which notice has been duly given, provided that a complaint, in writing, of conduct has been made.

    ii No person who has been expelled from membership shall be re-admitted except by a resolution carried by the votes of three quarters of the members present in person and voting at any general meeting of which notice has been duly given.

Borrowing powers

10 a The Co-operative shall have the power to borrow money for the

purpose of the Co-operative in whatsoever manner it may determine including the issue of loan stock.

b The Co-operative shall not receive money on deposit.

c The Co-operative may receive from any persons donations towards the work of the Co-operative.

d The Co-operative shall have the power to determine from time to time the terms upon which money is borrowed or loan stock is issued and to vary such terms and conditions subject to the provisions of sub-paragraphs (a) and (b) of this Rule.

Management of the Co-operative

11 a The management of the Co-operative shall be by regular general meetings (at least one every three months) at which all the members shall be present. It shall be called by the Secretary giving each member of the Co-operative seven clear days' notice of the date.

b Each general meeting shall elect a chairperson who shall have a casting vote in the event of a tied vote and whose function it is to conduct the business of the meeting in an orderly manner.

c A general meeting of members present shall constitute the committee of management and have the power to make decisions in accordance with the Rules of the Co-operative. The general meeting shall have the power to appoint and remove individuals and members.

d No business shall be contracted at any general meeting unless one half or 25 of the co-operative's members, whichever is less, are present throughout the meeting.

12 Every member present in person at a general meeting shall have one vote, resolutions will be decided upon a majority vote of all members present subject to Rule 11(b), except those to be decided in accordance with Rules 9 and 19(a).

13 An Annual General Meeting shall be held within three months of the close of the financial year of the Co-operative, the business of which will include:

a The receipt of the accounts and balance sheet.

b The appointment of the auditor.

c The election of a Treasurer under members' direction to be responsible for the proper management of the financial affairs of the Co-operative. The Treasurer shall hold office until the next Annual General Meeting unless removed from office by a general meeting.

d The election of a Secretary under the members' direction who will have those functions enumerated in these rules and such further functions as a meeting may determine. The Secretary shall hold office until the next Annual General Meeting unless removed by a general meeting.

14 The Co-operative may invest any part of its funds in the manner mentioned in Section 31 of the Act.

15 The Co-operative may appoint any one or more of its members to vote on its behalf at the meeting of any other body corporate in which the Co-operative has invested any part of its funds.

Application of profits

16 a No portion of the income of property of the Co-operative shall be transferred either directly or indirectly by way of dividend, bonus, or otherwise by way of profit to members of the Co-operative except insofar as the Agreement may provide upon surrender of shares.

   b The Co-operative may apply any profits towards carrying out the objects of the Co-operative.

   c Any profits not so applied shall not be carried forward.

17 a The Co-operative shall in accordance with Sections 4 and 8 of the Friendly and Industrial and Provident Societies Act 1968 appoint in each year one or more auditors to whom the accounts of the Co-operative for the year shall be submitted for audit.

   b Every year not later than the date provided for by the Act or where the return is made up to the date allowed by the Register, not later than three months after such date, the Secretary shall send to the Register the annual return in the form prescribed:

     i a copy of the report of the auditor on the Co-operative's accounts for the period included in the return and

     ii a copy of each balance sheet made during the period and of the report of the auditor on the balance sheet.

Minutes, books, seal

18 a Sufficient records shall be maintained and left at the Registered Office for the purposes of the Co-operative and to comply with the provisions of the Act.

   b The Co-operative shall have a seal kept in the custody of the Secretary and used only by authority of a general meeting. Sealing shall be attested to by the signature of two members and that of the Secretary for the time being.

Amendment of rules

19 a Any Rule herein may be rescinded or amended or a new Rule made by a vote of three-quarters of all members of the Co-operative present at a general meeting where all members of the Co-operative have been given seven clear days' prior notice of the proposed change.

   b No amendment of the Rules is valid until registered.

Dissolution

20 a The Co-operative may be dissolved by the consent of three-quarters of all the members by their signatures to an instrument of dissolution provided for by the Treasury regulations or by winding up in a manner provided by the Act.

 b Upon a claim being made by the personal representatives of a deceased member or trustee in bankruptcy of a bankrupt member to any property in the Co-operative belonging to the deceased or bankrupt member the Co-operative shall transfer or pay such.

 c A member may in accordance with the Act nominate any person or persons to whom any of his or her property in the Co-operative at the time of his or her death shall be transferred but such nomination shall only be valid to the extent of the amount of £1.00. On receiving satisfactory proof of death of a member who had made a nomination the committee shall, in accordance with the Act, either transfer or pay the full value of the property comprised in the nomination to the person entitled thereunder.

21 In these Rules the Act refers to the Industrial and Provident Societies Acts of 1965 to 1978 or any Act or Acts amending or in substitution for them for the time being in force.

Dru – 7 October 1998

Appendix B

Interview schedule

Section 1: This community and why you live here

1 Could you describe this community for me?
2 What made you decide to live in/found this community?
3 What, for you, is the most important thing about living here?

Section 2: Worldviews

1 What, if anything, do you think is wrong with modern society and politics?
2 What, if anything, would you like to see changed?
3 What do you think are the best ways to bring about social and political change?

Section 3: Intentional communities and political change

1 Do you think that intentional communities play any role in bringing about social and political change? Please explain.
2 Do you think that this community has a role to play in this?

Index